'This book provides unique insights into how practitioners should protect young children, drawing upon key theoretical and practice principles. The author identifies newer and more perverse forms of abuse affecting some children in their early childhood and proposes ways of working that are evidence informed and have the best interests of children at the fore. This is an essential text for students from a range of professional backgrounds with an interest in enhancing their practice with young children and their families, and the use of practice points and exercises bring the book's contents to life.'

– Dr Prospera Tedam, Anglia Ruskin University, Cambridge

'A most comprehensive, up-to-date text, which is suitable for all levels of professionals, practitioners, undergraduates and post-graduates in the field of early childhood. It is serious and well researched with appropriate theoretical frameworks, yet it is very readable and engaging. There are appropriate case studies and questions for reflection, which demonstrate a great understanding of humanity.'

– Carolyn Silberfeld, Chair Director,
Early Childhood Studies Degrees Network (ECSDN)

'This is a superb text for those new to the study of Early Childhood Education and Care (ECEC) and working in the field. There is an excellent focus on process but also the importance of effective communication with children, parents, colleagues and other professionals. The author emphasises the importance of non-judgemental reflective practice in a way that enables readers to understand the importance of their role in working with young children. This text offers an accessible, informative insight of this complex area.'

– Dr Damien Fitzgerald, Principal Lecturer, Department of
Education, Childhood and Inclusion, Sheffield Hallam University

Child
Protection
in the
Early Years

of related interest

Safeguarding Babies and Very Young Children from Abuse and Neglect
Harriet Ward, Rebecca Brown and David Westlake
ISBN 978 1 84905 237 5
EISBN 978 0 85700 481 9
Part of the Safeguarding Children Across Services series

Giving Children a Voice
A Step-by-Step Guide to Promoting Child-Centred Practice
Sam Frankel
ISBN 978 1 78592 278 7
EISBN 978 1 78450 578 3

Listening to Young Children, Expanded Third Edition
A Guide to Understanding and Using the Mosaic Approach
Alison Clark
Foreword by Peter Moss
ISBN 978 1 90939 122 2
EISBN 978 1 90939 126 0

British Values and the Prevent Duty in the Early Years
A Practitioner's Guide
Kerry Maddock
ISBN 978 1 78592 048 6
EISBN 978 1 78450 307 9

Promoting Young Children's Emotional Health and Wellbeing
A Practical Guide for Professionals and Parents
Sonia Mainstone-Cotton
ISBN 978 1 78592 054 7
EISBN 978 1 78450 311 6

Nurturing Personal, Social and Emotional Development in Early Childhood
A Practical Guide to Understanding Brain Development
and Young Children's Behaviour
Debbie Garvey
Foreword by Dr Suzanne Zeedyk
ISBN 978 1 78592 223 7
EISBN 978 1 78450 500 4

A Practical Guide to Gender Diversity and Sexuality in Early Years
Deborah Price
ISBN 978 1 78592 289 3
EISBN 978 1 78450 594 3

Child Protection in the Early Years

A Practical Guide

Eunice Lumsden
Foreword by Dr Celia Doyle

Jessica Kingsley *Publishers*
London and Philadelphia

First published in 2018
by Jessica Kingsley Publishers
73 Collier Street
London N1 9BE, UK
and
400 Market Street, Suite 400
Philadelphia, PA 19106, USA

www.jkp.com

Library of Congress Cataloging in Publication Data
Names: Lumsden, Eunice, author.
Title: Child protection in the early years : a practical guide / Eunice
    Lumsden.
Description: London ; Philadelphia : Jessica Kingsley Publishers, 2018. |
    Includes bibliographical references and index.
Identifiers: LCCN 2017060857 | ISBN 9781785922657 (alk. paper)
Subjects: LCSH: Early childhood education--Social aspects--Great Britain. |
    Abused children--Education--Great Britain. | Child welfare--Great Britain.
    | Child abuse--Great Britain.
Classification: LCC LB1139.3.G7 L86 2018 | DDC 372.21--dc23
LC record available at https://lccn.loc.gov/2017060857

British Library Cataloguing in Publication Data
A CIP catalogue record for this book is available from the British Library

ISBN 978 1 78592 265 7
EISBN 978 1 78450 555 4

Printed and bound by CPI Group (UK) Ltd, Croydon CR0 4YY

To Bill, Laura, Alex and Jackie

Acknowledgements

This book draws on nearly 40 years of working with children and families. Their individual and collective experiences have enriched my professional practice and continually reinforce the importance of a strengths approach to our work. Their stories inform every page of this book and remind us of our important role in enabling those who are facing adversity to shape a different future.

Thank you to Denise Hevey, Jane Murray and Robin Balbernie, who provided feedback, and to Celia Doyle, who has been a constant and critical friend throughout this process, and an inspiration throughout my career.

Disclaimer

All the case studies in this book are based on fictitious characters and stories, but do draw on real-life experiences. All information has been anonymised.

Contents

Foreword

Dr Celia Doyle

Young children are among the most vulnerable people in our community. Protected, cherished and encouraged to explore their world, they will flourish, but exploited, molested or subjected to violence or neglect, they will struggle to do so. Because Early Years practitioners relate so closely and for so many hours with young children, they are key professionals when it comes to safeguarding.

The essential role of Early Years staff was brought home to me during the many years I worked at the front line of child protection. I observed that they are the experts in communicating with pre-verbal children or those with limited verbal skills. Furthermore, every day they see lots of happy, thriving children, and so instinctively recognise one who, despite a cheerful façade, is neglected and suffering. Those involved in Early Childhood Education and Care (ECEC) can appear approachable and non-threatening, so parents experiencing difficulties with their children will feel comfortable confiding in them.

However, too often in the past staff engaged in ECEC had difficulty expressing their concerns or making their voices heard. I recall attending a case conference where the parents were absent.

The chairperson gave a young, female practitioner, introduced as a 'nursery nurse', very little opportunity to contribute, asking her to simply state whether the children attended nursery regularly. Before she could add anything else, the chairperson brusquely moved on to the other contributors. In the moments before the conference ended, the nursery nurse managed to mention that the mother had confided that she was pregnant again. Accordingly, just as everyone was preparing to leave, we all had to sit back down and spend another half an hour discussing the implications of this new development, given that it made many of our earlier recommendations irrelevant or inappropriate.

This example illustrates that while Early Years practitioners undoubtedly have superlative skills in observation, communication and in relating to young children and their families, some may need help and guidance to articulate their concerns or raise issues assertively with other professionals; *Child Protection in the Early Years: A Practical Guide* will assist with this. The book is designed to enhance basic knowledge of safeguarding and the impact of abuse on children's development. It will help ensure practitioners know how to recognise, record and report concerns. Readers are given insights into the relevance of attachment theory, the significance of policy and procedures, and the importance of working with others. Finally, the creation of an environment that promotes the development of traumatised children is discussed. There are exercises, reflection points, case studies and practice points, all designed to help readers assimilate information while the material is presented in a highly readable form.

Child Protection in the Early Years: A Practical Guide will prove a valuable resource in providing those working in ECEC with the knowledge and guidance to help them take full advantage of their skills and understanding in order to safeguard children.

Chapter 1

Introduction

Chapter objectives

By the end of this chapter you will be able to:

- Describe the importance of studying child protection in Early Childhood
- Know the key terms and pedagogical features included in the book
- Explain the theoretical framework
- Recognise the importance of being a 'safe practitioner'

Early Childhood is a unique period in human development, where the foundations for future health, wellbeing and learning are laid down. Infants and young children are totally dependent on the adults who care for them, and their rapid development is influenced by the environments in which they live. For those facing adversity, the importance of this period is magnified. Parents, caregivers and those who work in Early Childhood Education and Care (ECEC) settings should be sources of comfort and safety; however, for some infants and young children, this is not the case, as they are cared for by adults who place them at risk or who actually harm them. In fact, during the first five years of life, infants and young children are more likely to be harmed and to live in adverse environments where domestic violence, substance misuse or mental health are features (Department for Education (DfE) 2016a).

The central focus of this introductory text on child protection is to enable those studying Early Childhood or working in Early Years settings to appreciate the rights infants and young children have to:

- Be protected from harm
- Receive appropriate services and intervention if they are at risk of being harmed or have been abused
- Have practitioners and professionals working with them who understand the impact that adverse life experiences can have, and are able to apply this knowledge to their practice in ECEC.

This book provides an introduction to the complex and multi-dimensional area of child maltreatment, including legislation and policy that articulates that a child's needs must always be paramount (Children Act 1989; DfE 2015a; UNICEF 1989). It seeks to inspire you to want to know more and embrace your own responsibilities in this area. This includes recognising the importance of ongoing professional development and the importance of working from a strengths approach. Experiencing adversity in Early Childhood does not mean, as Balbernie (2017, p.7) rightly states, 'disaster'. Adults who choose to work with children and young people need to embrace every opportunity to promote the resilience factors that enable those who have faced adversity to develop skills to manage the challenges they may face throughout their life course.

This first chapter introduces the key terms used throughout the book, and considers how the professionalisation of the ECEC workforce brings new opportunities in this area of work. It also introduces the pedagogical features included in the book, and provides an overview of each chapter. Finally, it addresses the very important area of your own wellbeing, and how you need to ensure both you and your *practice* are 'safe'.

Key terms

Adverse Childhood Experiences (ACEs): This term has emerged from research in North America into factors that lead to later life health issues, such as obesity and diabetes. It is used to embrace the breadth of experiences from actual abuse to living in home environments where there is domestic violence and/or drug and alcohol misuse (see Chapters 2 and 5).

Adverse environments: This refers to the home environments that some children live in that can impact their holistic development. This includes, for example, poor housing, domestic violence, abuse, drug and alcohol misuse.

Child abuse/child maltreatment: These are used interchangeably throughout the book. They are umbrella terms that embrace all the categories of abuse (see Chapter 2).

Child protection: This is a generic term that includes legislation, statutory guidance, and local policy and procedures that have developed to protect or intervene when there are concerns about a child's safety (see Chapters 6 and 7).

Early Childhood: Over the last two decades the academic subject field of Early Childhood has become established as a distinct area of study with its own benchmark statement (Quality Assurance Agency (QAA) 2014). It is an inter-disciplinary subject that includes early learning, child development, child protection, and health and wellbeing. Throughout this book, 'Early Childhood' is used to embrace the holistic nature of the period from conception to the age of eight. It has been capitalised to reinforce this area as a distinct area of study and as a critical period in human development. The study of Early Childhood enables students to pursue a range of career options, including education, health and social care. The contents of this book provide the foundational knowledge in child protection for any of these career pathways. However, the practice points and case studies used aim to support the application of knowledge in ECEC practice.

Early Childhood Education and Care (ECEC): ECEC has been used in preference to other terms to highlight the equal importance of 'care' and 'education' in the Early Childhood period. Infants and young children face barriers to early learning if they are not appropriately cared for, their health and wellbeing is not prioritised or they are unsafe. ECEC also embraces the range of settings that provide early learning opportunities and care for infants and young children outside the family. These include childminding (home-based) and group settings. The latter encompasses the different types of provision available, including children's centres, pre-schools, nurseries, schools and pre- and after-school care.

Holistic childhood development/holistic development: These terms are used to reflect the importance of looking at all the developmental strands of the whole child that promote their optimal development in Early Childhood. These include social and emotional development, physical and cognitive development and health and wellbeing.

Key Person: The majority of ECEC settings employ a Key Person System. The Key Person is the name given to the practitioner who has responsibility for specific children attending the setting. They are the link person with the family (see Chapter 8).

Key Worker: Is the person who has lead responsibility for a Child Protection Plan that may be produced following a Child Protection Conference (see Chapter 6).

Nurturing care/environments: This refers to how infants and young children need to occupy spaces, whether in or outside the home, that are sensitive to their interrelated needs and holistic development. The global indicators of nurturing care in and outside the family are health, nutrition, safety and security, responsive caregiving and early learning (Black *et al.* 2017).

Parents/carers/caregivers: These terms are used throughout the book to describe those who are responsible for the primary care of the infant or child. This is not always the parents – it can be wider family members, foster carers or stepparents.

Professional and practitioner: While 'professional' and 'practitioner' are often used interchangeably, it is important to understand the difference between them:

- *Professional* refers to someone who has studied for a professional qualification or status. They are registered with a professional body and may have a code of practice and ethics to adhere to (Lumsden 2012; Taylor and Thoburn, 2016). There are recognisable characteristics associated with a profession that include:
  - Recognisable entry points – for example, with standard qualification requirements.
  - Codes of ethics – for example, that set out aspects of professional responsibility.
  - Systems for self-regulation – for example, setting and regulating standards for professional development.
  - A strong sense of vocation and professional development.
    (Panel on Fair Access to the Professions 2009, p.13)

Registration as a professional also brings responsibilities that include being answerable for their conduct in and outside the work environment as well as with individual clients/patients/service users, and they can be disciplined or even 'struck off' the register if they fail to meet the required standards of conduct or competence, or 'bring the professional into disrepute' (Taylor and Thoburn 2016, p.57).

- *Practitioner* is the term for those without registered professional status. They still have to work to the code of practice and guidelines of their employers and those included in the statutory frameworks that shape child protection practice in the United Kingdom (UK).

It is important to appreciate that both professionals and practitioners have significant contributions to make to the child protection process. For example, ECEC practitioners are skilled at observing children, and these observations provide a real insight into the child's world – these are invaluable contributions to the assessment process. However, the important point is that individuals, regardless of their role and qualifications, should not be working '...beyond their competency and for which they are not trained or adequately experienced' (Taylor and Thoburn 2016, pp.57–58).

Professionalisation: This term is used to refer to the upskilling of the ECEC workforce and the importance of those working in the sector practising professionally. It embraces the drive for a workforce that is able to apply knowledge to practice to improve individual outcomes.

Safeguarding: This is a broader term defined in the Children Act 2004 (Department for Education and Skills (DfES 2004), and embraces the importance of promoting the health and wellbeing of all children as well as protecting them from harm (see Chapter 6).

Setting the scene

This section considers why those studying Early Childhood and working in ECEC need to know about child maltreatment and ACEs. As Sally Davies, Chief Medical Officer, stated in the

Foreword to *The 1001 Critical Days*: 'Those who suffer multiple adverse childhood events achieve less educationally, earn less, and are less healthy, making it more likely that the cycle of harm is perpetuated, in the following generation' (Leadsom *et al.* 2013, p.2). In other words, we need to work with the *adult the child may become* rather than waiting to work with the *child in the adult*.

This knowledge is not new, and those who work in the child protection system understand the inter-generational cost of early trauma and the real challenges of intervening early to improve outcomes. In fact, over 40 years ago, Pringle and Naidoo (1975, p.169) argued:

> Though much remains to be learned about how to lay necessary foundations during the pre-school years, which will enable children to achieve eventually the fullest measure of their potential...enough is known to take some action now...promoting optimal emotional, social and intellectual development; preventing neglect and deprivation; and, most difficult of all, for breaking into the vicious circle of the emotional or intellectually deprived children of today becoming tomorrow's parents of yet another generation of deprived children.

What is different now is that there is burgeoning research evidence and powerful case studies from those who have faced trauma as children (Cherry 2013; Perry and Szalavitz 2017). Outcomes from successive serious case reviews (SCRs) (Sidebotham *et al.* 2016) indicate how child deaths repeatedly highlight system failures and communication difficulties between agencies as contributing factors.

Furthermore, the professionalisation of the ECEC workforce should bring optimism for the future. Early Childhood is now firmly established as an academic area, and child abuse and working with families, as well as multi-professional working, are integral to this area of study. This, alongside the development of graduate leaders and increased training and awareness in the workforce, should improve the early identification of child protection issues and intervention with infants, young children and their families.

Practice point: Policy and practice differences across the UK

It is important to add a cautionary note here. While this book argues that ECEC offers new opportunities, child protection is a complex area. There is no one answer to address the inter-generational challenges of child maltreatment: it requires an inter-disciplinary and multi-professional approach across the child's life span. Furthermore, there is not one consistent way of addressing child protection in the UK. England, Scotland, Wales and Northern Ireland have their own legislative frameworks, policies and procedures in relation to ECEC, safeguarding and child protection (see Chapter 6). It is important that you are aware of the specific requirements of the country in which you work.

Over the last two decades there has been increasing investment in workforce development in ECEC. In Scotland, for instance, those leading a setting must have, or be working towards, a degree in Childhood Practice (Scottish Social Services Council 2015). In England, Early Years Professional Status (EYPS) was introduced in 2007 (now called Early Years Teacher Status, EYTS). This graduate professional role and status in ECEC has a specific standard to meet in relation to safeguarding children from birth to five years of age (DfE 2013a). Furthermore, the *Childcare Act 2006* (DfES 2006) historically removed the divide between education and care in England and introduced the Early Years Foundation Stage (EYFS). This is the curriculum framework for the 0–5 age group, and includes important welfare and safeguarding requirements (DfE 2014). The policy drive for increased free childcare hours to support families back into work means that these requirements take on greater significance (GOV.UK 2017).

This ongoing professionalisation of the ECEC workforce brings with it new opportunities to work differently. Those working in the sector provide a largely untapped resource in the area of child maltreatment, especially in working with other professionals and focused work with infants and young children. However, one of the real challenges of the current system is a strong focus on procedures and multi-professional working. While these are of crucial importance, they can detract from actual work with infants and young children. The ECEC workforce has the potential to address this gap. They have a different kind of knowledge of and relationship with families using their settings. They also have holistic and intimate knowledge of infants and young children. Both of these are huge strengths to bring to the field of child protection, enabling contributions to the protection process as well as more focused approaches with infants and young children in their care (see Chapters 7 and 8).

However, despite ongoing investment in workforce development in ECEC, by the time young children reach statutory school age, the disadvantage gap is not diminishing (Family Care Trust and National Association for Head Teachers (NAHT) 2017; Office for Standards in Education (Ofsted) 2016; Stewart and Waldfogel 2017). For those working in ECEC and in the school sector, it is important to understand that the barriers preventing some children from achieving educationally are multi-faceted and influenced by wider societal factors, such as poverty and poor housing, as well as complex home environments (see Chapter 3). In other words, the term 'disadvantage' embraces a range of factors that are far wider than inappropriate parenting and child abuse. Moreover, it is not easy for families to change their circumstances. For example, the highest percentage of children living in the disadvantaged category of poverty is in working families (Tinson *et al.* 2016).

Theoretical frameworks

As you become more deeply embedded in the study of Early Childhood and child protection, you will find yourself constantly asking the question 'why?' Theories offer a lens to answer the 'why', a way of understand what is happening. In the area of child abuse, the 'why' questions could be about what makes an adult harm a child, why abuse is so difficult to identify and why it can result in lifelong problems, issues discussed later in Chapters 3, 4 and 5.

There are many different theoretical perspectives that facilitate an understanding of the complexities of child abuse and help to answer the 'why' questions, including ecological theory (Bronfenbrenner 1979, 1992, 2005). Bronfenbrenner's work (1917–2005) on the bio-ecological development of children cannot be underestimated. It has had a significant influence on our understanding of how complex factors at an international, national and local level, as well as events in the family, can influence a child's development. His work has influenced the assessment of children and families in need, discussed in Chapter 6, and provides the theoretical framework underpinning this book.

Bronfenbrenner's original work is usually presented as a set of nested circles, with the child in the centre (Bronfenbrenner 1979). Figure 1.1 provides a visualisation with each circle representing the systems that influence the child in order of their proximity:

- The *macrosystem* includes such things as national and international policy, culture and beliefs – these have an influence on all the systems. For example, in the area of child protection, legislation influences what happens with the agencies working at a local level in the *exosystem*. This, in turn, influences how agencies intervene with families in the *microsystem*.

- The *exosystem* does not always directly impact on the developing child but will interrelate with others in the *microsystem*. For example, the parents' workplace hours will influence the amount of time they require childcare. In the area of child protection, the local procedures of the organisations located in the *exosystem* define how they work with children and families in the *microsystem*.
- The *microsystem* is described as 'the complex of relations between the developing person and environment in an immediate setting containing the person' (Bronfenbrenner 1977, cited in Bronfenbrenner 2005, p.xiii). It comprises the interactive *mesosystem*, and different systems, relationships and experiences influence the child's development.

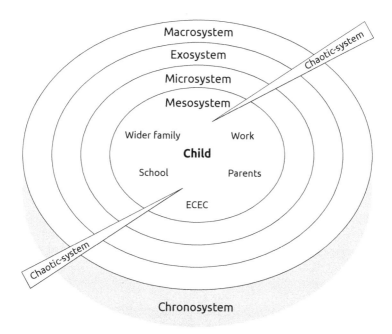

Figure 1.1: Bio-ecological theory with the chronosystem and chaotic-system

Bronfenbrenner (2005) recognised that his initial theorisation did not answer all the 'why' questions, and as a result he developed the *chronosystem*. This facilitates understanding of how experiences in the earliest years and one-off events can influence development over the life course. However, this raised further 'why' questions about the relationship between theory and real life. He became increasingly concerned with how 'chaos' in society, such as natural disasters or policy changes, impact on human development (Bronfenbrenner 2005). The *chaotic-system* (Lumsden 2012) offers another dimension to his theoretical framework, a lens that helps explain the impact of wider societal issues at a national level, on the community, family and a child's development (see Chapter 3).

Structure of the book and pedagogical features

Each chapter in this book specifically builds on the inter-disciplinary knowledge that underpins the practice skills required to work in the area of children protection and, more broadly, with infants and young children living in adverse environments. While the principle of a child's needs being paramount at all times is the same across the UK, there are variations between countries in law and practice. Wherever possible, the discussion highlights any differences and signposts you to country-specific information. Case studies that draw on anonymised real-life situation, exercises, practice and reflection points are used to deepen and extend understanding. There will also be suggestions of resources or further reading. These include a number of online resources. As web links can change over time, if the URL is no longer working, use the title and/or author in a search engine.

Chapter 2 is concerned with definitions and categories of abuse, how to recognise children at risk of abuse as well as barriers to detection. It also explores how to respond to disclosures and the importance of recording concerns and sharing them. You are also challenged to reflect on your own views about this emotive area.

Chapter 3 builds on this learning and focuses on the prevalence and causes of abuse. It will help you to understand the wider issues at a macro level that influence family life and lead to children being at risk of harm, or actually harmed. It emphasises that most parents and caregivers do not intentionally plan to harm their children – the stress of working, living on a low income and then a sudden event such as a bereavement could be contributing factors.

Chapter 4 specifically addresses the complex area of attachment. Those working in ECEC should have a good grasp of attachment processes and how to promote them in ECEC practice for *all* children. It is important to appreciate that children who have been abused or who live in adverse environments may have attachment issues, but not all children with diagnosed attachment difficulties have been abused.

Chapter 5 considers the impact of maltreatment and living in adverse environments on infants and young children, with a brief introduction to brain development and how early neglect and abuse can affect its development. ACE research is introduced, and there is a focus on the role of ECEC in the early identification of abuse and the importance of proactive intervention in working alongside children to develop resilience.

Chapter 6 introduces legislation, policies and procedures that inform child protection practice in ECEC across the four nations of the UK. It considers the stages of child abuse investigations, possible outcomes, how to refer concerns and your role in advocating for infants and young children. The range of assessments undertaken with families is also discussed.

Chapter 7 focuses specifically on the legal requirement for agencies and professionals to work together to protect children. It considers the contribution ECEC can make to multi-professional working, as well as the challenges and skills required in this area of work.

Chapter 8 addresses practice and the importance of developing nurturing environments that are sensitive to the holistic development needs of infants and young children, especially those experiencing early trauma. It introduces the Unique Childhoods Model, which offers a framework to critique, analyse and develop practice in ECEC to ensure infants and young children are visible at all times. There is also a focus on continuing professional development, with the concept of being a 'safe' practitioner introduced.

Chapter 9 draws the key threads of learning from the book together. It considers your own role and ongoing development in meeting the challenges inherent in working in the area of child abuse.

Taking care of yourself: The importance of being a safe practitioner

Child abuse is a challenging subject area that needs to be handled sensitively. With increased numbers of children accessing ECEC provision for longer periods of time, professionals and practitioners are more likely to work with infants or young children who are in need of safeguarding. It is an area where procedures need to be followed for your own safety as well as the child's. However, being involved with an infant or a child who has been abused, neglected or who lives in an adverse environment is emotive. For some, it can raise issues around their own childhood experiences. This is also true for other areas addressed in this book such as attachment and ACEs.

Exploring these areas can inevitably lead you to reflect on your own experiences and how your life course has been influenced. This process should be viewed positively, enabling you to understand yourself through a different lens, and enhancing your empathy for children and families. However, in order to listen effectively to infants, young children and families, you must listen to your own reactions, and seek help and advice if issues are raised for you or if you become distressed.

Useful resources

For advice and guidance
NSPCC, www.nspcc.org.uk/services-and-resources/nspcc-helpline
Provides online and telephone support, advice and guidance.
For online support: help@nspcc.org.uk; Tel: 0808 800 5000.

Further reading
Johnson, J. (2007) *Finding Your Smile Again: A Child Care Professional's Guide to Reducing Stress and Avoiding Burnout.* St Paul, MN: Redleaf Press. This book is based on experiences of working in North America, and addresses the challenges of working in caring professions with guidelines on how to manage stress and burnout.

Mainstone-Cotton, S. (2017) *Promoting Emotional Well-being in Early Years Staff: A Practical Guide for Looking after Yourself and Your Colleagues.* London: Jessica Kingsley Publishers. This book focuses on the importance of emotional wellbeing for those working in ECEC.

Chapter 2

Identifying and Responding to Child Abuse

Chapter objectives

By the end of this chapter you will be able to:

- Recognise the importance of safeguarding *all* children
- Define the different categories of child abuse
- Describe the signs of abuse
- Know how to record and report information
- Explain the importance of sharing concerns about children.

Introduction

It is really important that those working in ECEC understand the wider concept of safeguarding and know how to identify and respond to abuse and reporting procedures. This chapter presents the legal and official definitions of what is classified as a 'child', safeguarding children, child abuse and other categories of abuse. It challenges you to reflect on your own views, what has influenced them, and the fine line between punishment and abuse. There is a focus on the signs of abuse, how to recognise children who may be at risk of abuse as well as barriers to detection. How to respond to disclosures, record information and share concerns is also considered.

What is a 'child'?

Article 1 of the United Nations Convention on the Rights of the Child (UNCRC) defines a child as up to the age of 18 (UNICEF 1989). This definition is reinforced in the legislative frameworks in the four countries of the UK, and the safeguarding of children also covers the period to age 18. In England, for example, the documentation *Working Together to Safeguard Children* states that a child is:

> Anyone who has not yet reached their 18th birthday. The fact that a child has reached 16 years of age, is living independently or is in further education, is a member of the armed forces, is in hospital or in custody in the secure estate, does not change his/her status or entitlements to services or protection. (DfE 2015a, p.92)

However, while the legal age is 18, definitions of what is a 'child' vary depending on the context. There are global variations in, for example, the age of criminal responsibility, the age people can marry and the age of sexual consent. These are often younger than 18 years.

The period of Early Childhood is also defined by the UNCRC as up to the age of eight, taking into account all the development periods from birth and the global variations of when children start school (United Nations (UN) 2006). Young children are viewed as rights holders, including the right to be protected from harm.

Exercise: Child rights
- Write a list of the physical and emotional needs of young children who require protection.
- Turn this list into a list of rights.

Through our identification of a young child's physical and emotional needs, which include shelter, food and their need to feel secure, safe, a sense of belonging and being loved, their rights emerge. These include the right to caregivers and environments that keep them safe and meet their physical and emotional needs. Unfortunately for some children, the responsible adults (parents, carers and sometimes practitioners and professionals) in their lives harm them, physically, emotionally or through neglect. Some will also use children to meet their sexual needs or the needs of others and, increasingly, the online world makes children even more vulnerable to abuse. These experiences of early trauma can impact across the life course (see Chapters 4 and 5). Consequently, all those working with young children in ECEC settings and schools need to understand the importance of safeguarding, and the significance of creating safe and nurturing environments where children can thrive.

Defining child abuse

Safeguarding children

Formal definitions of keeping children safe have evolved from focusing purely on types of abuse (DH, Home Office and DfEE 1999) to differentiating between the broader aspects of promoting children's welfare, early identification and intervention, and protecting children from potential or actual abuse (DfES 2004). In England, *Working Together to Safeguard Children* (DfE 2015a) uses 'safeguarding and promoting the welfare of children' as an umbrella term, embracing:

- Protecting children from maltreatment
- Preventing impairment of children's health or development
- Ensuring that children are growing up in circumstances consistent with the provision of safe and effective care
- Taking action to enable all children to have the best life chances.

(DfE 2015a, p.92)

The Department for Education (DfE) has lead responsibility for safeguarding in England alongside other departments, including the Department of Health (DH), Home Office and Department for Work and Pensions (DWP).

Practice point: Policies and procedures

Each of the four nations of the UK produces its own policies and procedures for safeguarding and child protection guidance. These are updated regularly to reflect the changes in this very complex area of work (see Chapter 5 and the 'Further reading' section at the end of this chapter).

In the Early Years, the EYFS in England has specific safeguarding and welfare requirements. These stress the importance of creating 'high quality settings which are welcoming, safe and stimulating, and where children are able to enjoy learning and grow in confidence' (DfE 2014, p.16). Similar themes are in evidence in Northern Ireland, Wales and Scotland.

These requirements are important as they promote a proactive rather than reactive approach to the needs of young children. They should underpin practice that enables all children to maximise their life chances and to be able to transition through the different childhood development periods feeling safe, nurtured and loved. This will, in turn, enable the development of skills to manage the challenges that they will be presented with throughout their life course. We know achieving this for all children is aspirational rather than achievable. However, the professionalisation of the ECEC workforce and the introduction of graduate professionals should improve practice and outcomes for young children (see Chapter 3).

Exercise: Safeguarding in practice
- Make a list of how your work or a placement ECEC setting:
  - Welcomes visitors and children
  - Is safe for children
  - Supports children to enjoy learning and develop confidence
  - Could contribute further to good practice.

What is child abuse?

This section explores the factors that impact on how child abuse is defined. Before widening the discussion, it is important that you reflect on your current understanding of child abuse and what has influenced your views.

Exercise: What is child abuse?
- Write a short paragraph about what you think child abuse is.
- Compare your definition to that in the *Working Together to Safeguard Children* documentation in the quote below. How do they compare?

Reflection point
You may be an experienced practitioner who is reading this book to refresh or enhance your knowledge, or you may be at the start of your career. If this is the case for you, I cannot stress enough how important reflection is in this area of work, for your own wellbeing and for that of the children and adults with whom you work. Addressing how you really feel about issues will support your personal

and professional development in this complex area of work, whatever your role, and it will enhance your practice.

Consider the questions below so that you honestly reflect on your views and consider what has influenced them.

- What do you really know about child abuse and how have your personal experiences, training, experiences at work, school, the media – newspapers, social media and television – influenced your understanding of this area?
- What do you think about people who harm children?

These are two questions I revisit regularly, and I urge you to do the same. They ensure I keep abreast of changes in definitions, the nature of what is considered abusive, how public perceptions change and the factors that lead some people to harm children. Most importantly, they keep the child and their experiences central to my thinking.

Defining child abuse is challenging, and different cultures, societies and political ideologies have differing views on how the State should intervene in the lives of families and children (Munro 2008; Parton and Reid 2014). Furthermore, abuse is socially constructed, with definitions of abuse changing over time. Research and the findings of public inquiries into the deaths of children, abuse in institutions and in ECEC settings have shaped and deepened understanding and influenced policy and procedures (D'Arcy and Gosling 1998; Laming 2003; Plymouth Safeguarding Children Board 2010). For example, in ECEC settings, the *Little Ted's Inquiry* led to clear guidance and policy on the use of mobile phones by staff during work (Plymouth Safeguarding Children Board 2010).

The current working definition of child abuse in England, according to the DfE, is:

A form of maltreatment of a child. Somebody may abuse or neglect a child by inflicting harm, or by failing to act to prevent harm. Children may be abused in a family or in an institutional or community setting by those known to them or, more rarely, by others (e.g. via the internet). They may be abused by an adult or adults, or another child or children. (DfE 2015a, p.92)

This definition was first introduced in 2013 (DfE 2013b), and extended previous definitions by including 'via the internet', reflecting societal changes. The World Wide Web has led to the removal of certain barriers to abusers. It is now much easier to share images and information in a way that has increased the abuse of children online.

Reflection point

Is there a difference between justifiable chastisement and abuse?

There is a range of views on what constitutes abuse. Smacking is an excellent example:

- What do you think about smacking?
- When does a 'tap' become physical abuse?
- What has informed your view?
- Do you know what your colleagues think about this subject?

Answering these questions is not easy, and your responses and those of others will be impacted on by training levels, experiences in the work setting and personal experiences within the family and in the institutions in which you have been involved, as well as by the media.

Cultural practices highlight differences in how the physical chastisement of children is viewed. For example, several European countries, including Sweden, Cyprus, Finland, Denmark and Norway, have banned the smacking of children by parents, whereas, until recently, successive governments in the UK have decided against passing legislation that makes the smacking of children illegal. In some circumstances, hitting a child has been seen as reasonable or justifiable chastisement, despite the UK being a signatory to the UNCRC (UNICEF 1989), which clearly argues in Article 19 that there should be legal and administrative structures to protect children from parents and carers, and that children should not be physically punished (UN 2012).

There is also clear research evidence of the possible long-term impact of physical punishment, and that it can quickly escalate to actual physical abuse (Heilmann, Kelly and Watt 2015). It is the ongoing research evidence, alongside their quest to make Scotland the best place for children to grow up in, that has led to the Scottish Government commitment in October 2017 to support a Private Members' Bill to ban smacking (Scottish Parliament 2017).

Exercise: Smacking
- Research what the current legislative situation is in Scotland, with the smacking ban:
  - What were the factors that led to a smacking ban being proposed in Scotland?
  - What has happened since it was proposed in 2017?
  - How have England, Wales and Northern Ireland responded to the situation in Scotland?
- What do you think are the implications about physical chastisement and physical abuse for the training of those working in ECEC?

In England, the *Childcare Act 2006* (DfES 2006) clearly states that there is a duty in Early Years to ensure that staff are supported to know the signs of 'potential abuse and neglect' (DfE 2015a, p.56), and there is a trained lead for safeguarding (see Chapter 5). It is important to recognise that, while settings must provide training and support, those working in the sector have a responsibility for their own development, as will be discussed later, in Chapter 8. Practitioners need to be able to recognise the signs of abuse, respond to changes in a child's behaviour, physical appearance and wellbeing, and listen to what children tell them, both verbally and non-verbally.

Types of abuse

Having considered the complexities of child abuse, this chapter now addresses how to support your understanding of the different types of abuse and how they interlink.

> **Exercise: Types of abuse**
> - Write a list of the types of abuse you are aware of.
> - Write your own definition for each.
> - How do your list and definitions compare with those described in Table 2.1?

According to the DfE, there are four main types of abuse (see Table 2.1), and their definitions have not remained static. In fact, if the policy definitions over the last ten years are interrogated, shifts in the social construction of abuse are clearly evident. Current English definitions, also evident in the other nations of the UK, embrace societal changes that have resulted in new areas deemed to be abusive. For example, cyberbullying is now included, and the definition of sexual abuse has been broadened to include imagery and grooming online. In 2017 a separate category of 'child sexual exploitation' was added, and emotional abuse now includes children who are overprotected and those not able to engage in appropriate learning. All these areas are explored further in Chapter 3.

Table 2.1: Definitions of child abuse

Physical abuse	A form of maltreatment. Somebody may abuse or neglect a child by inflicting harm, or by failing to act to prevent harm. Children may be abused in a family or in an institutional or community setting by those known to them or, more rarely, by others (e.g. via the internet). They may be abused by an adult or adults, or another child or children. It is a form of abuse that may involve hitting, shaking, throwing, poisoning, burning or scalding, drowning, suffocating or otherwise causing physical harm to a child. Physical abuse may also be caused when a parent or carer fabricates the symptoms of, or deliberately induces, illness in a child.
Emotional abuse	This is the persistent emotional maltreatment of a child such as to cause severe and persistent adverse effects on the child's emotional development. It may involve conveying to a child that they are worthless or unloved, inadequate or valued only insofar as they meet the needs of another person. It may include not giving the child opportunities to express their views, deliberately silencing them or 'making fun' of what they say or how they communicate. It may feature age or developmentally inappropriate expectations being imposed on children. These may include interactions that are beyond a child's developmental capability, as well as overprotection and/or preventing the child participating in normal social interactions. It may involve seeing or hearing the ill treatment of another. It may involve

	serious bullying (including cyberbullying), causing children frequently to feel frightened or in danger, or the exploitation or corruption of children. Some level of emotional abuse is involved in all types of maltreatment of a child, although it may occur on its own.
Sexual abuse	This involves forcing or enticing a child or young person to take part in sexual activities, not necessarily involving a high level of violence, whether or not the child is aware of what is happening. The activities may involve physical contact, including assault by penetration (e.g. rape or oral sex) or non-penetrative acts such as masturbation, kissing, rubbing and touching outside of clothing. They may also include non-contact activities, such as involving children in looking at, or in the production of, sexual images, watching sexual activities, encouraging children to behave in sexually inappropriate ways, or grooming a child in preparation for abuse (including via the internet). Sexual abuse is not solely perpetrated by adult males; women can also commit acts of sexual abuse, as can other children.
Child sexual exploitation	This is a form of child sexual abuse. It occurs where an individual or group takes advantage of an imbalance of power to coerce, manipulate or deceive a child or young person under the age of 18 into a sexual activity: (a) in exchange for something the victim needs or wants, and/or (b) for the financial advantage or increased status of the perpetrator or facilitator. The victim may have been sexually exploited even if the sexual activity appears consensual. Child sexual exploitation does not always involve physical contact; it can also occur through the use of technology.

Neglect	This is the persistent failure to meet a child's basic physical and/or psychological needs, likely to result in the serious impairment of the child's health or development. Neglect may occur during pregnancy as a result of maternal substance misuse. Once a child is born, neglect may involve a parent or carer failing to: provide adequate food, clothing and shelter (including exclusion from home or abandonment); protect a child from physical and emotional harm or danger; ensure adequate supervision (including the use of inadequate caregivers); or ensure access to appropriate medical care or treatment. It may also include neglect of, or unresponsiveness to, a child's basic emotional need.

Source: DFE (2015a, pp.92–93)

In addition to these areas of abuse, other categories not officially defined in the *Working Together to Safeguard Children* document include the following:

Domestic violence: The latest definition of domestic violence used by all government departments in England and mirrored in Northern Ireland, Wales and Scotland is:

Any incident or pattern of incidents of controlling, coercive, threatening behaviour, violence or abuse between those aged 16 or over who are, or have been, intimate partners or family members regardless of gender or sexuality. The abuse can encompass, but is not limited to:

- psychological
- physical
- sexual
- financial
- emotional.

(Home Office 2016, lines 8–18)

It is also a form of emotional abuse when children see or hear the ill treatment of another, for example, children seeing a parent being maltreated. For the Early Childhood period, domestic violence within the family can impact on the unborn child, brain development, attachment and early learning (Sterne and Poole 2010).

Institutional and system abuse: It is important to acknowledge that children can experience abuse in the institutions they are part of and by the system that is trying to protect them (Beckett 2007; Kay 2003). For example, there are historic cases of child abuse in residential homes. Furthermore, the abuse experienced by some children makes them vulnerable to further abuse.

Faith or belief abuse: With changing patterns of migration, different methods have emerged in childrearing practices associated with faith or beliefs. There is limited literature in this area, but we do know that over recent years there has been increased awareness of black children, especially those with a disability, experiencing abuse associated with spiritual possession and witchcraft (Bernard and Harris 2016; DfE 2007; Laming 2003; Simon *et al.* 2012; Tedam and Adjoa 2017). Simon *et al.* (2012, p.14) defined this area as including:

- Abuse that occurs as a result of a child being accused of witchcraft or of being a witch
- Abuse that occurs as a result of a child being accused of being 'possessed by spirits' – that is, 'spirit possession'
- Ritualistic abuse
- Satanic abuse.

While the actual numbers of reported cases are relatively small, it is believed that there is considerable under-reporting, and that cases go undetected (Bernard and Harris 2016). Witchcraft labelling can lead to emotional and physical abuse and neglect, and the consequences for children can be severe (Tedam and Adjoa 2017).

Female genital mutilation (FGM): This requires a special mention as it is a significant safeguarding issue and is illegal in the UK. FGM is a particular form of physical abuse. The procedure is undertaken on girls from birth, and it is an important area for those working in ECEC and in the health services to be aware of. It involves 'a procedure where the female genitals are deliberately cut, injured or changed, but where there's no medical reason for this to be done' (National Health Service (NHS) 2017a, lines 1–3). Historically, there have been attempts to justify or ignore FGM as a long-established cultural practice in certain communities, but it is now recognised that FGM can cause long-term serious physical and psychological damage for which there can be no legitimate justification.

Recognising abuse

This section explores signs and indicators of abuse to support your understanding of why abuse goes undetected. It is important to recognise that, regardless of experience or role, identifying child maltreatment is not straightforward. As Doyle (2014, p.229) rightly states, 'Even experienced paediatricians and other medical specialists find it difficult to determine the cause of many injuries, even with the help of sophisticated X-ray and other equipment'.

Reflection point

If you worry about missing the signs of abuse, you are not alone. This area of work is particularly challenging, regardless of experience or profession.

- Make a list of your concerns, and speak to a colleague or another student about their concerns.
- Are they different or similar?
- What will support you to manage your concerns?
- What support do you think your workplace should provide?

High-quality initial training, ongoing professional development and supervision are vital for the safeguarding of children as well as for practitioners' wellbeing. Furthermore, the role of the Key Person for children attending ECEC settings is fundamental to promoting the welfare of all children (Elfer, Goldsmeid and Selleck 2012; Johnson 2016). It is the quality of the relationships between the setting and the Key Person with the child and their family that promotes safeguarding and the child's wellbeing. The observations and communication skills of practitioners are therefore crucial in recognising when 'something is not quite right'. The importance of this cannot be underestimated in the Early Years. This is because of the number of developmental stages very young children transition through, and their dependency on the adults responsible for their holistic development including their care needs and safety. Consequently, practitioners need to be skilled in recording their observations, which must be clear, concise and factual, and avoid generalisation and hearsay.

Early Years practitioners work alongside pre-verbal and verbal infants and young children, who do not always have the vocabulary or understanding to articulate what is happening to them, or know that it is wrong. They may actually see themselves as a 'naughty child' who makes the adult act in the way they do. Young children are unlikely to make a 'one-off disclosure': they are more likely to present a picture over a period of time. Emotional abuse and neglect are particularly challenging to identify (Doyle 2012). Practitioners need to be able to recognise the other cues children provide through their behaviour, physical appearance and conversations:

Verbal: If the child is able to talk, they may say things that alert you to something happening within the home, for instance, 'Daddy hit Mummy', 'Mummy is sad' or 'Mummy hurts me'.

Behaviour: This can manifest itself in many different ways. The behaviour of the child may change suddenly or over time;

they may become aggressive to other children, staff and resources in the setting. They could appear withdrawn and anxious or may fluctuate between extremes of emotions. They might present as hungry and tired or play inappropriately with other children. They may also speak or act in ways that mirror what is happening to them outside the setting.

Physical appearance: There may be a change in how a child is dressed; you may notice unusual bruising or the child may wince when touched. They may have difficulty walking, standing or sitting as well as being in pain. There may be burn or bite marks.

Attendance: There may be unexplained or unexpected absences from the setting or a pattern of missing sessions. They may also be frequently late to sessions or their parent or caregiver late in collecting them.

Practice point: Supervision

The EYFS (DfE 2017a, p.21) highlights the importance of supervision, stating that it should provide opportunities to 'discuss any issues – particularly concerning children's development or wellbeing; identify solutions to address issues as they arise and receive coaching to improve their personal effectiveness'.

- What do you think is the role of supervision in the area of safeguarding?
- What are the arrangements for supervision in your workplace or on your practice placement?
- Does the setting have a supervision policy?
- What are the barriers to providing supervision in ECEC settings?

What to do if you are concerned about a child, or practice, in the setting

It is really important that all those working with children and families are alert to potential or actual abuse (DfE 2015b). If you have any concerns about a child, or practice, you *must* follow the policies and procedures of your setting. Childminders also have procedures in place that should involve direct referral to Children's Services. If you are a student, you need to follow the procedures of your practice setting and those of your training provider, college or university. Chapter 6 focuses specifically on legislation and policy and procedures.

If a child discloses abuse, the most important thing is to listen to the child and pass no judgement. Let them know what you will be doing and follow your workplace procedures. It is important you record what you have been told as soon as you can and as accurately as possible. However, as indicated earlier, young children are more likely to present a picture over a period of time. Their distress is often expressed non-verbally, and developing a picture over time, through accurate observations and record keeping, is essential. It is also important to discuss your observations and concerns with the relevant person in the setting.

CASE STUDY: MICHAEL

Michael is just over two years old. He is the youngest of three children and attends your setting for 15 hours per week. There have been general concerns about his physical appearance: his clothes do not fit properly – they are either too small or too large. Sometimes he is dressed inappropriately for the weather; for example, he is in a thick jumper when it is hot. Michael often arrives hungry and tends to go straight to the snack area. He has been observed hitting other children.

Michael also has speech delay and there are concerns about his hearing. The setting has been working closely with the health visitor and speech and language therapists.

There has been a sickness bug in the setting and Michael has not attended for a week. On his return he seems quieter than usual and takes longer than normal to settle. You have to change his nappy and notice five marks, each about the size of a penny, that look like bruises that are fading on the side of his leg, at the top.

- What do you think are the issues for Michael?

Concerns about Michael's physical presentation and development have already been noted. The marks on the top of his leg are concerning – they could be fingertip bruising, indicating he had been hit. Although the bruising is suspicious, there could also be a clear explanation of what happened to cause them.

It is vital not to make judgements; rather, you should discuss the situation with the designated person is the setting for child protection and follow the safeguarding procedures as soon as possible or contact Children's Services if you are a childminder.

Chapter summary

This chapter has illustrated the importance of having a good understanding of the differences between safeguarding children and promoting their welfare and child abuse. It has highlighted the fine line between punishment and abuse, and the challenges in identifying abuse, as well as acknowledging the challenging and emotive nature of this area of work and the impact it may have on yourself and other workers. Understanding of policies and procedures is vital, as well as ongoing training and support.

Key learning

- The period of childhood is considered up until the age of 18.
- Safeguarding is an umbrella term capturing the promotion of environments that support children to be safe and to develop.
- Child protection is about protecting children from abuse.
- Categories of abuse are not static; they change over time.
- The systems for addressing safeguarding and child protection are different across the four nations of the UK.

Useful resources

For advice and guidance

Should Sarah Smack Her Child?, www.nottingham.ac.uk/nmp/ sonet/rlos/sociology/sarah
This eLearning activity, which you can do alone or with others, explores the complexities and ethical issues of corporal punishment. Sarah is a single mother who has just started a new relationship. Her new partner believes she is too lenient with her daughter and should smack her more. The learner is supported to think about their own views in light of family, stakeholders and professional opinions.

National Society for the Prevention of Cruelty to Children (NSPCC), www.nspcc.org.uk
There is excellent advice on this website, which covers England, Wales, Scotland and Northern Ireland in relation to all aspects of child abuse.

NHS on FGM, www.nhs.uk/conditions/female-genital-mutilation/Pages/Introduction.aspx

NSPCC on FGM, www.nspcc.org.uk/preventing-abuse/child-abuse-and-neglect/female-genital-mutilation-fgm/legislation-policy-and-guidance

England: Early Years, www.gov.uk/topic/schools-colleges-childrens-services/early-years

England: Child protection, www.gov.uk/topic/schools-colleges-childrens-services/safeguarding-children

Scotland: Early Years, https://beta.gov.scot/policies/early-education-and-care

Scotland: Child protection, https://beta.gov.scot/policies/child-protection

Wales: Early Years, http://gov.wales/topics/educationandskills/allsectorpolicies/welshmededuca/early-years-pre-school-education/?lang=en

Wales: Child protection, http://gov.wales/topics/health/socialcare/safeguarding/?lang=en

Northern Ireland: Early Years, www.education-ni.gov.uk/articles/early-years-education

Northern Ireland: Child protection, www.health-ni.gov.uk/topics/social-services/child-protection

Further reading

Burton, S. and J. Reid (2014) (eds) *Safeguarding and Protecting Children in the Early Years*. Abingdon: Routledge. This is an edited book that develops many of the areas introduced in this text.

Bernard, C. and Harris, P. (2016) *Safeguarding Black Children: Good Practice in Child Protection*. London: Jessica Kingsley Publishers. This book challenges those working in the child protection area to improve practice with black children.

Chapter 3

The Importance of Understanding Child Abuse in Early Childhood Education and Care

Chapter objectives

By the end of this chapter you will be able to:

- Explain the prevalence of child abuse
- Discuss the causes of abuse, including the impact of domestic violence, mental health and substance misuse
- Recognise the factors that lead to child abuse in ECEC settings.

Introduction

This chapter discusses the prevalence of child abuse as well as the preconditions that can lead to children being maltreated. The estimated numbers of children suspected or known to have been abused are considered, and the chapter introduces different theoretical perspectives that help to explain why abuse occurs. The chapter also focuses specifically on the wider adverse life experiences that contribute to abusive situations, which include domestic violence, mental health issues and substance misuse. The final section draws on two cases of child abuse in

ECEC settings where SCRs were conducted, and considers the implications for practice.

Prevalence of child abuse

The exact number of children, especially young children, facing adverse experiences in childhood is unknown, and only a small percentage is received into local authority care. The majority of abused children continue to live with their families; some have had professional involvement, others have ongoing involvement and some families go undetected. The NSPCC has argued that the number who are actually at risk of harm is at least eight times the number who are placed on a Child Protection Plan (see 'Practice point' below) because of risk of abuse or because they have been abused (Harker *et al.* 2013).

Practice point: Child Protection Conference and a Child Protection Plan

A Child Protection Conference takes place when there are concerns about the potential for abuse or when abuse has occurred. A Child Protection Plan can be drawn up after the Conference to outline the support plan for the family, identify the Key Worker and the core group of professionals involved, as well as actions to be taken and to set the review date. In Scotland, Wales and Northern Ireland a decision is also made as to whether to place the child's name on the Child Protection Register (see Chapter 6).

Every year, England, Scotland, Wales and Northern Ireland publish data about the characteristics of children under their respective legislation who are deemed to be 'in need'. This information includes those with a disability or other additional needs, those subject to Child Protection Plans and those who are living away from their families or who are adopted. The year-on-year trend in relation to incidents of child abuse and neglect that are known about is slightly upwards, as is the number of children on Child Protection Plans and 'looked after' by local authorities (Bentley *et al.* 2016). Furthermore, the data clearly indicate that, while initial referrals to Children's Services may be because of suspected abuse, at the end of the assessment period, domestic violence, mental health and drug and alcohol misuse are identified as major contributing factors.

Spotlight on statistics

Drawing on English data, this section considers in greater detail the characteristics of children who are deemed 'in need' or where abuse is suspected or has occurred. Of the approximately 11.5 million children in England, data from the period 1 April 2015 to 31 March 2016 (DfE 2016a) state that 571,640 children were referred for assessment under the *Children Act 1989* and 394,400 children were deemed 'in need'. The largest group continued to be children aged 10–15, while 93,230 (23.6%) were under five years old. About half of the referrals (50.6%) were because of concerns about abuse, although by the end of the assessment other factors emerged. In 49.6 per cent of cases children were living in families where domestic violence was prevalent, mental health issues were found in 36.6 per cent of cases, and in a further 19.3 per cent of cases, there was drug misuse and in 18.4 per cent alcohol misuse.

As a result of these assessments, 50,310 children then became subjects of Child Protection Plans. Of these, 19,820 involved children under five and 14,810 children aged 5–9. Neglect was the primary reason for a plan recorded in 44.9 per cent of cases; in a further 35.3 per cent of cases, emotional abuse was the primary reason for a plan.

Focusing specifically on the Early Childhood period, 3,431,000 children were aged 0–4 in 2015–16 (Office for National Statistics (ONS) 2016). Of these, 7840 unborn babies were deemed 'in need', 4530 because of abuse and neglect and 1020 were on a Child Protection Plan. Another 11,760 under the age of one were deemed in 'in need' because of abuse and neglect and 5080 were on a Child Protection Plan. A further 42,690 children aged 1–4 were in need because of abuse and neglect and 13,720 were on Child Protection Plans.

Table 3.1 provides a 'snapshot' of the reasons why children were initially on a Child Protection Plan.

Table 3.1: Number of children who were the subject of a Child Protection Plan as of 31 March 2016, by age and category of abuse

	Unborn	Under 1	1–4	5–9	10–15	16 and over
Total no of children[1] who were the subject of a Child Protection Plan at 31 March 2016	1020	5080	13,720	14,810	13,810	1870
Neglect	660	2740	6490	6400	6050	810
Physical abuse	100	530	1190	1210	1030	150
Sexual abuse	20	170	420	600	960	210
Emotional abuse	200	1430	4910	5740	4920	570
Multiple[2]	50	210	710	860	860	130

Source: DfE (2016a)

1. All figures are rounded to the nearest 10.
2. 'Multiple' refers to instances where there is more than one main category of abuse. These children are not counted under the other abuse headings, so a child can appear only once in this table.

Reflection point
- What do you think about these statistics?
- Do they surprise you?
- Are they higher or lower than you expected?
- What do you think about the numbers of infants suffering abuse under the age of one year?
- What do you think about the types of abuse young children have experienced?
- What do you think the implications of the statistics may be for practice in ECEC?

Practice point: The relevance of child abuse statistics to ECEC

The data discussed in this section has highlighted the prevalence of child abuse. Despite increased knowledge and expertise in this area, very young children continue to face considerable adverse traumatic experiences in the Early Childhood period, which have potentially lifelong implications. Not only are they in danger of abuse, or have been abused, they also live in environments characterised by domestic violence, mental health issues and drug or alcohol misuse.

It is important that assumptions are *never* made; rather, practitioners require ongoing training in safeguarding and the wellbeing of *all* children. There are three reasons for this:

- An increasing number of young children attend ECEC settings.
- Most children facing adverse life experiences live with their families.
- Not all children who experience disadvantage are abused, although millions of infants and young

children live in families where poverty presents barriers to wellbeing and life chances.

It is through high-quality ongoing training that those working in ECEC will appreciate the importance of applying theoretical knowledge to practice, rather than knowing the specifics of individual situations. Children and families have a *right* to confidentiality and a workforce that appreciates how enabling environments can support babies and young children to develop the brain architecture and building blocks to support their holistic development. This is achieved through a professionalised workforce that knows the child, their family and the community, and so is able to address the collective, as well as the unique, needs of every child.

Understanding the causes of abuse

Trying to make sense of why some people harm children is important for all those working with children and families, not only to prevent abuse happening in the first place, but also to 'give a greater sense of control to the worker over events that might otherwise seem inexplicable' (Corby, Shemmings and Wilkins 2012, p.131). In ECEC, it is increasingly important that the workforce develops a greater understanding of this area. Furthermore, the importance of reflection and supervision to address feelings evoked by the complex and challenging lives experienced by some young children and their families cannot be underestimated.

While abuse can and does take place outside the family, including in ECEC settings, the majority of children, especially very young children, are abused in the privacy of their family. They are harmed by people they know: their mothers, fathers, siblings or wider family members. There are no definite reasons why some people abuse and others do not, and abusers come from all areas of society. Moreover, different families can face similar challenges that can lead to abuse in one family but not in another. Mothers are more likely to be responsible for physical abuse, emotional abuse and neglect, primarily because they are usually the main caretaker. Men are usually, but not exclusively, the perpetrators of sexual abuse, and female children rather than males tend to be the victims, although this is not always the case (Corby *et al.* 2012; Sterne and Poole, 2010).

In short, understanding the causes of all types of abuse and what makes some people abuse a child is an extremely complex issue. There is no one clear type of abuse, abuser or reason. There is no checklist; rather, a number of factors have been identified that result in families being deemed 'vulnerable' and in need of support. These include marital conflict, unwanted pregnancy, mental health, drug and alcohol dependency, previous experience of abuse, unemployment, low income and poor housing. However, changes in family structure, cultural diversity, globalisation and the internet have further complicated the area of child protection. Therefore, theoretical frameworks to support an understanding of the causes of child abuse take on greater significance. For example, Bronfenbrenner's work, discussed in Chapter 1, provides a framework for understanding how events in the macro- and exosystems can impact on the family.

The work of the late Brian Charles Corby (1946–2007) is also invaluable here. He identified three broad theoretical perspectives that help us comprehend why some people abuse children (Corby 2006, p.156; Corby *et al.* 2012, p.132):

- *Psychological theories:* those that focus on the instinctive and psychological qualities of individuals who abuse.
- *Social psychological theories:* those that focus on the dynamics of the interaction between the abuser, child and immediate environment.

- *Sociological perspectives:* those that emphasise social and political conditions as the most important reason for child abuse.

These theoretical perspectives facilitate greater understanding of abuse in relation to specific situations. For example, psychological theories indicate that there may be predispositions to abuse because of early deprivation or other factors such as experiencing domestic violence. Alternately, social psychological theories suggest the immediate environment can lead to maltreatment occurring, for example, because of the interplay between an unwanted pregnancy, domestic violence, unemployment and poor housing. The sociological perspective would perceive this same situation as the interplay between the State, the impact of policies and the social conditions of the family.

Another perspective that supports understanding of the reasons for abuse is how *power* is used. Anti-discriminatory practice acknowledges the power we all have; it is how it is used that is the important factor for abuse. Parents, or those caring for young children, are in positions of power; their role is to support, protect and teach until those children are independent. However, one of the defining features of maltreatment is when '...at least one person, usually a parent figure...is misusing the power they have over the child' (Doyle 2014, p.225). Doyle (2014) contends that abuse can occur not only at the micro level of the family, but also at national and international levels against particular groups or countries. She has also identified three pre-conditions that can lead to abuse.

First, where people abuse or misuse the power they have; second, where victims are objectified '...either at an individual level when abusers fail to see the essential humanity of their victim, or at a societal level such as occurred during the slave trade when "slaves" were viewed as commodities' (Doyle 2014, p.225). Finally, is when people are silent witnesses and do not recognise or appreciate the seriousness of different situations. They may also be 'co-victims too frightened to disclose; or associates of the abuser who gain vicarious pleasure from the victim's suffering' (Doyle 2014, p.225).

An underpinning rationale for this book is to ensure that ECEC is not unwittingly an intentional 'silent witness' because of practitioners' lack of understanding of child abuse. A second rationale is the significance of those who work in ECEC as partners with health, social care and police colleagues.

Reflection point

Think about someone you have power over.
- How do you exert that power?
- How do you feel when you exert your power?
- How do you think the other person feels?

Think about someone who has power over you.
- How do they exert that power?
- How do you feel when they exert their power?
- How do you think the person exerting the power feels?

You may have exerted power in a positive way that supported the person and vice versa. However, when power is used negatively, these questions may evoke a range of intense feelings that you have learnt to manage over time. The important point here is to understand that a child will not understand or have the language to verbally express how they are feeling. Therefore, understanding how young children express feelings through their behaviour is important (see Chapter 4).

CASE STUDY: TOBY AND NADINE

Samantha (21) has two children by different fathers, Toby, aged three-and-a-half, and Nadine, aged two. Both attend nursery for 15 hours per week. Samantha was adopted as a young child, having suffered neglect as a baby. She has a reasonable relationship with her adoptive parents, and they continue to support her emotionally and financially.

Samantha became pregnant at 17 but did not tell anyone until she was six months pregnant, and did not appear to know who the father was. Samantha's relationship with Nadine's father, Simon, was volatile, and the police were called regularly because of suspected domestic violence linked to alcohol and drugs.

Simon had a history of drug dealing and, on the same day the police arrested him, Samantha received a notice of eviction from her house for non-payment of rent. The next day she took both children to the nursery and admitted to hitting Toby, leaving a bruise on his face. She said he would not do what he was told and she just lashed out.

Exercise: Apply theory in practice
- Consider how each of the theoretical perspectives presented by Corby and Bronfenbrenner can help you understand why Samantha has harmed Toby.
- What role has the misuse of power played in this case?
- How do you think having some understanding of the causes of abuse will support your work?

Practice point: The importance of understanding why abuse happens

Child abuse is a complex subject and is evident in all sectors of society globally. It is vital that those working in ECEC settings understand that there are multi-faceted causes for abuse, and conclusions should not be drawn from limited information. Practitioners need to remain professional at all times, share and record concerns, and avoid informal conversations about families that may lead to judgemental comments and stereotyping abusers.

In this case study, Samantha is a young mother with two very young children by different fathers and with complex relationships. Her earliest experiences were of neglect, which can impact on all aspects of development and across the life course (see Chapter 5). She continues to be supported by her adoptive parents. This situation does not necessarily mean that the children are being abused. Samantha is under considerable stress, a situation that may have led her to respond to Toby's behaviour by inappropriately smacking him. Actually, at the time of writing this book, smacking a child in the UK is not against the law, although this was about to change, as is already the case in Scotland (see Chapters 2 and 6). However, this family is vulnerable to abuse occurring because of the dynamics of the adult relationships, where power appears to be being misused, alongside alcohol- and drug-related issues and police involvement. Furthermore, there are financial issues leading to the non-payment of rent and possible eviction.

The ECEC setting has an important role to play in supporting the family and other professionals working with them. Most importantly, they are powerful advocates for infants and young children. The holistic knowledge of the child and their development provides an invaluable contribution to any multi-professional assessment being undertaken (see Chapter 6). The ECEC environment provides rich opportunities for quality play experiences that focus specifically on social and emotional as well as cognitive development, communication and fine and gross motor skills. Finally, ECEC provides a crucial opportunity to work alongside parents or primary caregivers to enhance their understanding of their child's development needs and the importance of the home learning environment.

Specific issues that contribute to abuse

This section addresses specific issues in the lives of adults that can lead to children being abused, physically, emotionally, sexually or through neglect. As Ventress (2014, p.79) states: 'Parental mental health, substance misuse and domestic violence have become known by the chilling epithet "the toxic trio" because they feature so commonly in families where child abuse takes place'. Analysis by Sidebotham *et al.* (2016) of SCR, conducted when a child is seriously harmed or killed, highlights that domestic violence was an issue in almost half of the cases, as was drug and alcohol misuse. Furthermore, and of vital importance for those working in ECEC, all the reviews conducted between 2003 and 2014 have highlighted two distinct groups of children who are at risk of domestic violence: young adolescents and those from birth to school age. Pregnant women are also at high risk of violence from their partners, who can have an adverse impact on the unborn baby (Sterne and Poole 2010). However, as Sidebotham *et al.* (2016, p.239) point out:

> Although there is emphasis on the deleterious effects of neglect on the youngest children and their developing brains, the age group where neglect is most prominent in serious case reviews is among young people aged 11–15, where the impact of neglect over many years becomes apparent.

This situation reinforces the importance of those working in ECEC identifying and supporting families early, and having a deep understanding of how domestic violence, mental health and substance misuse can be pre-conditions to child abuse.

Domestic violence

The exact causes of domestic violence, also referred to as domestic abuse, are multiple but are fundamentally about power and control, with the abuser using a range of threats and violence to control (Sterne and Poole 2010). There are numerous myths about why domestic violence occurs (Refuge 2017), and addressing the issue is not simple. Drugs and alcohol misuse can fuel violence, but cannot and should not be used as an excuse for behaviour that stems from the need to control. 'Coercive control' has been clearly identified by the *triannual review of SCRs (2011–14)* as an important issue in domestic violence in families, and is now illegal. Another key factor identified is that domestic violence *is* child abuse (Sidebotham *et al.* 2016). This is collaborated by the statistics presented at the start of this chapter that found in nearly 50 per cent of needs assessments, which had been undertaken because of suspected abuse, domestic violence was identified as the primary causal factor (DfE 2016a).

While women can be instigators of domestic violence, the perpetrators are usually men, but can come from all parts of society. Domestic violence can occur in any type of relationship, including both heterosexual and same-sex partnerships. It usually goes on in the privacy of the home and is often a 'family secret'. While adults who are violent to each other may not necessarily be physically violent to children, they do expose them to volatile situations, which can lead to emotional abuse and their classification as being at risk of significant harm (see Chapter 6). Moreover, as Sterne and Poole (2010) point out, where there are oppressive and abusive relationships, the atmosphere in the home can be one of 'tension and fear' and 'women are most vulnerable to extreme violence at the point of separation, when her partner realises that he is losing control of her' (Sterne and Poole 2010, p.15).

Separation does not necessarily end the violence or fear of it. If the family has moved from the area to be protected, the perpetrator may continue to try and find them. There are women and children in refuges around the country who are in fear of being found. Furthermore, as Iwi and Newman (2011) point out, it is very unlikely for a court not to agree to formalised contact between children and the offending parent. This brings with it further opportunities where the welfare of children may be compromised and the potential for emotional abuse heightened.

Practice point: Domestic violence

When I started my career as a social worker in the early 1980s, domestic violence was not seen as a child protection issue, yet I was frequently involved with families where the impact on the children was evident. The power of the perpetrators over the victims was also evident, and I was often involved in supporting women to move in to a refuge, only to find they had returned to their partner within days. For women from minority ethnic families there were, and continue to be, added challenges of pressures from the 'community' not to bring shame on the family name.

Despite legislation and the welcome shift in perceptions that children living in environments where there is domestic violence are victims of abuse, there is still no national strategy in England for addressing domestic violence. Moreover, it is left up to charities to provide support, and many are struggling for funding. However, there is so much that can be done in ECEC settings to make them 'domestic abuse aware', while providing a safe haven and environments where children can be nurtured.

Exercise: Domestic violence
- Make a list of what the implications of domestic violence are for ECEC settings and your own practice with children and families.

For those working in ECEC, it is essential to understand that domestic violence impacts on all the family, and there are strong links with neglect and the emotional abuse of children. Practitioners have a vital role in the detection, referral and support of young children.

It is not easy for victims of abuse to recognise it is happening in the first place, and actually having the strength to leave the perpetrator is difficult. Moreover, as discussed earlier, if there are children involved, it is difficult to be totally free of the abuser. Additionally, the situation is compounded by a lack of formalised services and an over-reliance on charitable organisations as being responsible for supporting those entangled in domestic abuse. Nevertheless, ECEC settings can provide nurturing environments that are sensitive to an individual child's needs, by ensuring planning is appropriate for a child who is living in a volatile home situation. Settings should also ensure that there is information that is visible about local support for victims.

Mental health

Mental health is another complex multi-faceted area that can also embrace drug and alcohol misuse. The causes of mental illness are manifold and range from hereditary causes to environmental factors, or a combination. They can include psychotic illnesses such as bipolar disorder or schizophrenia, obsessive compulsive disorders, and depression and anxiety. Treatments can be effective and assumptions should not be made that having a mental illness equates with poor parenting. However, the consequence of having one or more parents with mental health issues can adversely impact on the children in the family, especially as the foundations for mental health are laid down in early childhood (Beckett 2007; Center on the Developing Child 2013, 2016; Ventress 2014).

Abuse as a child can lead to mental health issues in childhood and as an adult. Research indicates that women who have been abused have a greater chance of experiencing pre- and postnatal depression (APPG Conception to Age 2 2015). In the 2010 version of *Working Together to Safeguard Children*, the Department for Children, Schools and Families (DCSF) (2010, p.268) states that research evidence implies that children whose '...mothers who have mental ill health are five times more likely to have mental health problems themselves'. Risk factors are greater for children if mental illness coexists with other issues such as drug and alcohol misuse (Cleaver, Unell and Aldgate 2011). In some cases, as identified in the ongoing SCRs (Sidebotham *et al.* 2016), mental illness can lead to serious injuries and fatalities.

The importance of maternal mental health and the impact on the child of depression in the perinatal period (conception to one year old) is well known. Over the last few years, this area and wider issues about infant mental health have gained prominence at policy level. Campaigning by groups such as the Maternal Mental Health Alliance has supported the inclusion of perinatal mental health as a target area in *Next Steps on the NHS Five Year Forward View* (NHS 2017b). It is important that those working in ECEC know about this aspect because not only do ECEC settings have baby rooms, but they also have contact with expectant mothers. Unfortunately, the mental health of the mother not only impacts on the infant's development, but could also mean that the infant is at risk of abuse, or is being abused.

It is important to note that fathers can also experience mental health issues following the birth of a baby.

The impact of early trauma in early childhood is explored further in Chapter 5.

Drug and alcohol misuse

The impact of alcohol and drugs on the unborn baby and subsequent development of infants and young children's lives cannot be underestimated. Alcohol and drugs, whether they be legal, illegal or prescribed, as well as nicotine, are, as Beckett (2007) reminds us, in common use, and there is considerable controversy about addiction and dependency. Assumptions should never be made that their presence leads to poor parenting; it is only when they impact on parenting that the protection of children becomes an issue.

As the statistics at the beginning of this chapter illustrate, in the period 1 April 2015 to 31 March 2016 (DfE 2016a), drugs were evident in 19.3 per cent and alcohol in 18.4 per cent of 'child in need' assessments. These figures have changed little over time. In 1999, Cleaver *et al.* suggested that about 20 per cent of initial referrals were for drug and alcohol misuse. However, these figures relate to children who are known about. In their series *All Babies Count: Spotlight on Drugs and Alcohol* (Rayns, Dawes and Cuthbert 2013, pp.6–7), the NSPCC analysed the national Psychiatric Morbidity Survey (NHS 2007), and found that in England, around:

- 79,000 babies under one are living with a parent who is classified as a 'hazardous or harmful' drinker – this equates to 93,500 babies in the UK
- 26,000 babies under one are living with a parent who would be classified as a 'dependent' drinker – this equates to 31,000 babies in the UK
- 43,000 babies under one are living with a parent who has used an illegal drug in the past year – this is equivalent to 51,000 across the UK
- 16,500 babies under one are living with a parent who has used Class A drugs in the past year –this is equivalent to 19,500 across the UK.

What the data suggest is that substantial numbers of young children are living in families with drug and alcohol misuse, and that the figures coming to the attention of professional services have varied little over the last 20 years. Furthermore, the number of babies affected pre-birth and in the first year of life is substantial. We know that if women drink in the prenatal period, this impacts on the foetus's brain development, and in the first trimester, on the central nervous system. Babies can be born with foetal alcohol spectrum disorder (FASD) or foetal alcohol syndrome (FAS). Both can affect an individual across the life course, impacting on their behaviour, physical development and cognitive abilities.

According to the All Parliamentary Party Group (APPG) on FASD (APPG 2015), it is not until children with FASD move up the education system, from around the age of six, that the impact on their cogitative abilities become more pronounced. However, the APPG on FASD report (2015) suggests that it is from around the age of six that the impact on children's cogitative abilities becomes more pronounced. However, it is the impact of ongoing parental alcohol misuse on parenting capacity in the Early Years that can have a profound effect on children. According to Rayns *et al.* (2013), it can result in neglectful, negative and inconsistent parenting. This situation is compounded if there is drug misuse and domestic violence, and professionals should take action to safeguard children from the long-term effects of neglect and emotional abuse (Humphreys and Bradbury-Jones 2015; Sidebotham *et al.* 2016).

The impact of drug misuse on women and children is immense, and during pregnancy drugs can pass through the placenta to the growing child. According to Rayns *et al.* (2013, p.7), drug taking can lead to '...spontaneous abortion, congenital malformations, low birth weight, poor growth and premature delivery'. Babies diagnosed with neonatal abstinence syndrome, in other words, those who have to be withdrawn from drugs, display 'irritability (high pitched crying, inability to sleep) and gastrointestinal symptoms (poor feeding, regurgitation, poor weight gain)' (Rayns *et al.* 2013, p.7). However, the exact number of children living in families where illicit drug use is an issue is difficult to know as by its very nature it is illegal, and therefore secrecy is inherent (Cleaver *et al.* 2011). Furthermore, while there appears to be limited longitudinal research into the impact of drug misuse, it is believed that addiction to drugs negatively impacts the ability to parent, leading to neglect, poor attachment and lack of responsiveness to the baby's needs (Cleaver *et al.* 2011).

Reflection point

The causes of child abuse are multi-faceted and complex.

- What do you think about the causes of child abuse?
- Do they surprise you?
- How do you think knowing about these will impact on your practice?

Abuse in Early Years settings

Before concluding this chapter, we move away from a discussion on family issues of domestic violence, mental health and substance misuse to recognise that not all abuse happens in families or is caused by parents. While Disclosure and Barring Service (DBS) (2017) checks are in place to support safe recruitment, abuse of all types does occur in ECEC settings, and it is essential that procedures are in place to ensure that any allegations are taken seriously and acted on (see Chapter 6). Practitioners need to be able to recognise and have the confidence to report situations that may lead to a child being unsafe.

Reflection point

Do you know what your setting or training providers' policies are for reporting concerns about abuse?

Were you given training on reporting concerns about abuse as part of your placement preparation or induction to your job?

SCRs, where abuse has already occurred, provide excellent insights into circumstances that make children vulnerable to abuse in settings. Two of the most recent reviews are the *Little Ted's Inquiry* (Plymouth Safeguarding Children Board 2010) and *Little Stars Nursery* (Wonnacott 2013). Both cases involved sexual abuse and highlighted the preconditions that contributed to the abuse taking place:

- Poor leadership and management
- Careless staff recruitment
- Lack of appropriate safeguarding training
- Concerns about the standard of practice by the local authority
- Concerns expressed by students not being acted on
- Proper checks of students not undertaken
- Staff relationships
- Lack of boundaries in relationships with parents.

Exercise: Protective environments
- Consider each of the preconditions that led to the sexual abuse of children in these two nurseries, and write a list of the actions you think could have been taken to address them.

These two cases emphasise that for infants and young children to be 'safe' when they are being cared for outside the family, they need ECEC environments where there is:

- Strong leadership
- Ongoing safeguarding training
- Strong attention to safeguarding and welfare procedures and policies
- Clear procedures for the use of social media by staff and with parents
- Careful attention to recruitment, references and DBS checks.

Chapter summary

The chapter has highlighted that not all children who are abused, in danger of being abused or living in adverse environments are known to the authorities. While most abuse occurs in families, it can happen in ECEC settings, and those working in the sector need to know the required procedures and need to take action if they have concerns about their colleagues. The causes of child abuse are multi-faceted, and it is important not to be judgemental, but rather to recognise the vital need to apply theoretical knowledge to practice. Those working in ECEC are key people in the early detection of abuse or situations where children may be in danger of being harmed. They also have an important role in contributing to multi-professional assessments, creating rich ECEC environments and working alongside families.

Key learning

- The exact number of children being abused or living in adverse environments is not known.
- The number of children who do come to the attention of the authorities because of safeguarding issues varies little year on year.

- The causes of abuse are multi-faceted.
- Abuse usually occurs when a number of factors come together.
- Infants and young children's holistic development can be impacted on by maltreatment and/or living in adverse environments.
- The majority of children who are abused continue to live with their families.
- Children are usually abused by their parents or caregivers, within their families.
- Children can also be abused outside the home, by strangers and in institutions, including ECEC settings.

Useful resources

Further reading
Rayns, G., Dawe, S. and Cuthbert, C. (2013) *All Babies Count: Spotlight on Drugs and Alcohol*. London: NSPCC. Available at www.nspcc.org.uk/globalassets/documents/research-reports/all-babies-count-spotlight-drugs-alcohol.pdf. This short but comprehensive report from the NSPCC highlights the impact on babies of parental addiction. It not only presents data about the extent of the problem, but also preventative and intervention measures.

Sterne, A. and Poole, L. (2010) *Domestic Violence and Children: A Handbook for Schools and Early Years Settings*. Abingdon: Routledge. A practical guide for those working in the Early Years and school settings aimed at improving practice with children who experience the consequences of living in environments with domestic violence.

Chapter 4

An Introduction to Attachment Theory

Chapter objectives

By the end of this chapter you will be able to:
- Explain the importance of attachment theory in ECEC
- Discuss the complexity of attachment theory
- Differentiate the various classifications of attachment
- Outline the role of caregivers in promoting attachment.

Introduction

All infants and young children have a right to adults who are sensitive and responsive to their needs. They require parents and carers who provide a 'secure base' from which they learn about themselves and how to relate to others. Attachment theory is the study of these processes, and it is a complex and constantly evolving area of study. For those working with children and families, understanding the different theoretical perspectives on attachment processes as well as knowledge about how the brain develops is crucial. This chapter is specifically concerned with providing an introduction to attachment theory, and Chapter 5 then focuses on the developing brain and the impact of adverse life experiences on an infant and young child's development. However, it is important to note here that attachment processes and the developing brain are interconnected. This chapter also addresses contemporary perspectives on the processes that promote positive attachment behaviours and the importance of sensitive, attachment-aware ECEC environments that provide nurturing care.

Understanding attachment

Since the original work of Bowlby (1955, 1969, 1988), research into attachment processes continues to provide an insight into how our earliest experiences, especially in the first two years of life, influence later life outcomes. More recently there has been a shift towards understanding attachment in relation to emotional as well as cogitative learning and, with this, interpersonal neurobiological models of attachment have emerged (Schore 2014a). Researchers have drawn on the social and biological sciences to enhance understanding of attachment processes and their role in human development (Barlow *et al.* 2015; Barlow 2017; Moullin 2017). With the increasing knowledge in this area there has been recognition of the need for a multi-professional approach to individuals and families where secure attachment has not occurred, especially where subsequent maltreatment is a possibility (Balbernie 2017). Consequently, the range of intervention strategies with children and families has also increased.

Policy direction focusing on reducing workless families and women being encouraged to work is leading to younger children attending ECEC for longer periods of time. Consequently, an appreciation of ongoing research into attachment processes is essential for all those studying and working in Early Childhood. It is important to note here that professionals often talk about attachment and bonding together, but they are different.

They are not interchangeable terms – an attachment is a more specific term relating to the attachment processes that take place between the infant and the caregiver that facilitate the infant becoming attached to the primary caregiver and the primary caregiver developing the 'caregiving bond' (Wilkins, Shemmings and Shemmings 2015, p.24).

In the first few years of life, the need for an attachment relationship and the organisation of the processes involved in forming this are biological. However, the quality of the attachment relationship, to which both caregiver and baby contribute, is dependent on real-life experiences. In neurological terms, forming an attachment is experience-expectant and the final outcome is experience-dependent. It is through the process of caring and nurturing for the infant that the bond between the primary carer and the infant develops – an intense emotion of 'love' develops. However, the nature of this bond can be complex, especially if the attachment that develops between the infant and the caregiver is not secure.

From birth, babies need to feel safe and secure, and develop close and secure attachments to their primary caregiver, usually their mother. The Center on the Developing Child at Harvard University reinforces that while parents are the primary attachment figures, young children '...can also benefit significantly from relationships with other responsive caregivers both within and outside the family' (Center on the Developing Child 2017a, p.1). They also highlight the importance of babies and young children needing 'nurturing and reliably available adults' to support the attachment process.

Attachment stems from the primary caregiver being able to understand the baby's cues and respond to their needs. Usually, but not always, attachment behaviours occur when a baby feels threatened or anxious in some way, in other words, when the baby is in a state of high arousal (see Figure 4.1). Attachment behaviour is only observed when the perception of threat has activated the attachment system, and for the majority of a child's day, this should not be visible.

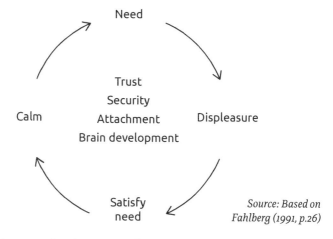

Figure 4.1: The arousal–relaxation cycle in developing attachment

The model (see Figure 4.1) provided by Fahlberg (1991) in her seminal text for children placed for adoption supports a basic understanding of how attachment is developed after birth. The baby experiences a physiological or psychological need and uses crying to get attention. The caregiver responds to the baby's need, for example, comforting the baby, feeding them or changing a nappy. The baby quietens, relaxes and feels safe. The main factor is the sensitivity of the carer to the baby's needs, and it is this cycle that facilities 'trust', 'attachment' and 'security' – what has become known as a 'secure base' (Ainsworth *et al.* 2015; Bowlby 1988; Fahlberg 1991; Howe 1998, 2005; Schofield and Beek 2006; Wilkins *et al.* 2015). It is a cycle that also facilitates brain development.

The four basic attachment behaviours that initiate the attachment cycle are now commonly known as:

- Secure base effect
- Safe haven
- Proximity seeking
- Separation protest.

Practice point: Attachment behaviours

An interesting way to understand the four basic attachment behaviours has been put forward by Hazan and Zeifman (1994). They suggest that we all need someone:

- Who is there for us – a *secure base*.
- To whom we turn when we need support and comfort – a *safe haven*.
- Whom we want to be with – *proximity seeking*.
- Whom we do not like to be separated from – *separation protest*.

Reflection point

Think about these in relation to your attachment figures.

- Have these changed over your life course?
- How many people fulfil all four roles for you?
- How do you think these questions can be used to address the needs of infants and young children attending ECEC settings?

It is through the development of the 'secure base' that the growing infant develops their internal model for understanding the world, named by Bowlby (1969, 1988) as the *Internal Working Model*. This comprises three components: a model of self, a model of *the other* and a model of the relationship between the two. The 'secure base' is there to deactivate the attachment system, allowing the child to explore, play and be creative, whereas the 'safe haven' aspect of the Internal Working Model epitomises the child's (often unconscious) expectations of comfort and reassurance if the attachment system kicks into action. If the baby has been responded to in a way that ensures their needs are met, they feel safe and begin to explore their environment, knowing their parent or caregiver is there for comfort and will respond to their needs. This working model is not fixed; rather, it can be adapted and expanded, supporting the infant and child to develop an attachment with others.

More recently, our understanding of this Internal Working Model has been extended to appreciate how human interaction mediates between human biology and individual psychology and the structure of the brain. This has resulted in greater understanding of how the infant's brain adapts to its environment. The 'plasticity' of the brain is, according to Balbernie (2013, p.212), 'at its most responsive and adaptable phase of growth in the first 2–3 years of life where its basic architecture' is constructed. The really important point here is that it is the quality of the relationship with the caregiver(s) that impacts on the structure of the brain and later life relationships (Schore 2014a). Therefore, attachment is not just about how an infant relates to itself and others; it is also about how they think and feel. In other words, emotional wellbeing starts in the first year of life through non-verbal communication between the baby and their primary caregiver.

It is through the processes of falling in love, nurturing and interacting that parents and caregivers develop their sensitivity, becoming attuned to the needs of the infant, learning how to respond and developing a concept that has been termed 'mentalisation' or 'mind-mindedness'. This process is when the parent or caregiver tries to understand how the baby is seeing the world in terms of internal processes of the mind. These include feelings, beliefs, attitudes and expectations (Howe 2005; Schofield and Beek 2006). The process that promotes secure attachment should lead to '...better outcomes in social and emotional development, educational achievements and mental health [and] are thought to be crucial for alter social relationships and for the development of capacities for emotional and stress regulation, self-control and mentalisation' (National Institute for Health and Clinical Excellence (NICE) 2015, p.44). However, as Balbernie (2015) points out, parents can display sensitivity to the needs of the infant but respond inappropriately. He argues that what is important is the carer's ability to see the infant as having their own mind.

It is also important to note that, while there are cultural differences in parenting patterns, research indicates that regardless of background, babies will form an attachment with a small number of caregivers (Wilkins *et al.* 2015). This is also true of the four basis attachment behaviours, previously identified, which are evident in all cultures (Shemmings and Shemmings 2011). Cultural differences can be found, however, in how emotions and behaviours are displayed, and how children are socialised in this area. For example, there are different cultural practices when a baby is born or when a family member dies.

As the baby grows, the caregivers and infant relationship deepens and the positive interaction cycle develops (Fahlberg 1991). Figure 4.2 provides a useful visualisation, and it is through the endless daily repetitions of this cycle that the development of 'satisfying reciprocal relationships' begin that have '...a physiological effect on the neurobiological structure of the growing child's brain that will be enduring' (Balbernie 2013, p.210). This is often seen in rhythmic patterns between the caregiver and infant – what Hughes (2006) describes as a 'dance' or the Center on the Developing Child (2016) as 'serve and return'. This process is natural in families where parents are attuned to their baby's growing needs. It is through this cycle that the brain's architecture develops and the infant's sense of self and emotional wellbeing (Schore 2014a). The infant begins to develop the skills of regulating their behaviour and emotional responses. This process requires social-emotional skills and cognitive processes to work together (Moullin 2017).

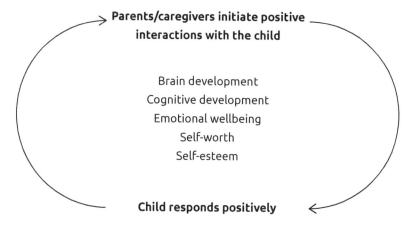

Source: Based on Fahlberg (1991, p.30)

Figure 4.2: The positive interaction cycle

There is also a claiming process that takes place as part of this process, where the child becomes part of the immediate and wider family. However, claiming does not always take place, by the parent or the wider family. Balbernie (2017) has identified some of the risk factors including low birth weight, disabilities, parental mental health, addiction, family history of dysfunction, abuse and loss, domestic violence, and low income and inadequate housing.

In some families, therefore, external factors act as barriers to parents being available to the infant or young child, or they may be inconsistent in their responses to the baby's distress. Furthermore, as Balbernie (2017, p.6) goes on to argue, '...multiple problems impacting an infant in the first two years of life pretty well predict that the child without intervention, will grow up struggling with emotional and cognitive adversity that will be a disadvantage in all areas of life'. For example, the Internal Working Model developed by the infant may be one of being unable to predict what will happen to them when they are distressed.

Practice point: The importance of attachment figures

The importance of an infant's attachment to their primary caregivers, usually their parents, cannot be underestimated. Infants and children are at the centre of a wider network of caregivers, including grandparents, siblings and those working in ECEC. Secure attachments are formed with those who respond sensitively to their needs, with infants and young children learning about themselves and others. The more often they care for the infant and child, the more likely the child is to turn to them at times of stress. However, frequent changes or loss of those providing care impacts on the ability to trust and to make sense of relationships with others.

It is important that those working in ECEC, whether as childminders or in group care, recognise their part in the wider community, 'claiming' the infant and young child, making them feel secure and safe in the environment. Consequently, practitioners need an understanding of:

- The importance of the 'secure base' and responding to all four basic attachment behaviours
- 'Mind-mindedness/mentalisation' and the importance of practitioners trying to understand the world through the eyes of the infant or child
- The significance of attachment for emotional wellbeing as well as cognitive development
- The impact of changes in staff and the significance of more than one Key Person.

Types of attachment

When the infant experiences relationships that are unresponsive, lacking in emotional warmth, that do not meet their basic needs or are abusive, brain development can be affected. It is argued by some researchers that this can lead to different patterns of attachment emerging that have been labelled: 'avoidant attachment', 'ambivalent or resistant attachment' and 'disorganised (or controlling) attachment' (see Table 4.1) (Balbernie 2013; Wilkins *et al.* 2015).

These categorisations originally emerged from the work of Ainsworth on the *Stranger Situation procedure* (Ainsworth *et al.* 1978). There is no doubt that her work has been influential, although some commentators have questioned the ethics of the Stranger Situation experiment and the cross-cultural relevance of the categories that emerged (see, for example, Doyle 2012; Doyle and Timms 2014; McKenna 2009). Research suggests that there is a 60/40 divide between 'secure' and insecure' attachment behaviours in different cultures (Shemmings and Shemmings 2011; Wilkins, Shemmings and Corby 2012). A review of evidence on interventions in the Early Years aimed at improving attachment found that '...only two thirds of children are securely attached and that disorganised attachment has a prevalence of 15–19% in population samples; up to 40% in disadvantaged populations and as many as 80% in maltreated populations' (Barlow *et al.* 2015, p.12).

Table 4.1: Contributing factors and types of behaviour in attachment types

Type	Contributing factors	Types of behaviour
Secure attachment	This develops when the infant is in a sensitive and nurturing environment where they feel safe, secure and supported in making choices. They feel able to explore the world. Their social and emotional development is promoted, which, in turn, develops self-esteem, self-efficacy and confidence. In other words, a secure attachment suggests the infant will develop to have good levels of outcomes in all areas. This does not mean that they will not face challenges that could impact on their physical and psychological development across the life course. However, if they develop a secure attachment in early childhood, they are more likely to have the skills (resilience) to cope with adversity. They also are more able to process, express and manage their feelings.	As the infant develops they begin to explore the world, knowing if their caregiver is absent that they will return. The key point is that as infants and young children explore their world, they are displaying exploratory behaviour rather than attachment behaviour. The latter is only evident when they face some form of threat. As they move through childhood they begin to be able to make relationships, become dependable and able to depend on others. They develop a good sense of self and move towards independence as an adolescent and into adulthood.

Insecure attachment	This area is often considered in relation to the four categories of disorganised, avoidant attachment, ambivalent or resistant attachment. Disorganised attachment behaviours are most commonly associated with child abuse.
Avoidant attachment	This occurs when the caregiver experiences difficulty or is unable to sensitively meet the infant's needs. They have been unable to be sympathetic or offer comfort at times of distress.	As the infant develops they avoid close relationships and minimise their own feelings so as not to upset their caregiver or face rejection. The avoidant child finds ways to meet their own needs. As they move through childhood they may appear to be compliant; however, they are working very hard behind the scenes to manage their feelings and not to show them.
Ambivalent or resistant attachment	Often results due to inconsistent or lack of nurturing parenting; in other words, the child's needs are met but the infant cannot work out how the caregiver will respond to them. Their distress is either ignored or responded to, but not always positively.	As the infant moves through developmental stages they can display behaviours to make them noticed. For example, they can be loud, demanding, clingy and also distrustful because they are never sure what response they will receive. In adulthood, the word 'preoccupied' is often used to refer to those identified with this attachment type. They may be dependent on others but are also anxious that others do not care about them.

Type	Contributing factors	Types of behaviour
Disorganised attachment	This is when the primary caregiver has so many issues of their own they are unable to meet the needs of the baby on any level. This is the attachment type usually associated with abuse, and can impact on the child's internal workings, leading them to harm others. One of the most important characteristics of this type of abuse is fear for the person who is the caregiver, for example, in cases of domestic violence. This fear is often referred to as 'fear without solution'.	There may be a range of behaviours presented by a child with disorganised attachment. Research suggests that it may only be visible for short periods when they are frightened of or for their caregiver. At these times they may, for example, run to their primary caregiver but stop before they get there, to check whether they are being welcomed or not. They may cry for their caregiver or avoid them. At other times their behaviour will be indistinguishable from others. The long-term consequences can be physical ill health, mental ill health and particular conditions such as depression, personality disorders or attention disorders.

Source: Adapted from Balbernie (2013); Schofield and Beek (2006); Shemmings and Shemmings (2011); Wilkins et al. (2015)

Table 4.1 has specifically avoided lists – how a child is attached is not, and should not, be seen as a checklist. Furthermore, these categories should not be accepted as static – attachment is complex and influenced by numerous factors including context, environments and cultural practices. Assessing attachment is difficult, and what we see in a specific interaction may not be the truth and usually requires a multi-professional approach. It may be more useful to closely observe the child's behaviour in situations where one would expect the attachment system to be activated, as well as thinking about their capacity for emotional or affect regulation. For example, assumptions cannot be made that a child playing closely by their primary caregiver and not wanting to leave them is securely attached. It may be that they are anxious about how their parent will respond to them because of inconsistent care or abuse.

Other complex processes may be taking place. For example, Doyle (2012, 2014) describes *Stockholm Syndrome* as a complex process first noted in a bank robbery in Sweden where those held hostage were more afraid of the police than those who had held them captive. Doyle (2012) considers this in relation to child maltreatment, arguing that children experiencing abuse can go through a process akin to grief and loss. They move through stages of denial, fear, anger and depression. They may also have to learn to manage 'psychological contrast', a situation where one parent is abusive and the other tries to be kind. Therefore, to others, the family is not seen as a cause for concern.

Practice point: Attachment and child maltreatment
Attachment must be seen as one part of the holistic development of an infant and child, and a factor to be assessed in child maltreatment. Regardless of experiences within the family, children usually display loyalty to their parents. Even when children are abused by their parents or caregivers, they are still attached to them.

Furthermore, children with a secure attachment with their parents are not immune from abuse or psychological challenges across the life course. As Chapter 3 evidenced, the causes of abuse are multi-faceted. Additionally, not all infants or young children who have attachment difficulties or who have been maltreated repeat the same patterns when they become parents.

It is important, however, to realise that not all parents or caregivers actually love their children. They may meet the child's basic needs for food and shelter, but do not provide loving, nurturing experiences that promote secure attachments. The reciprocal dance between the parent and the infant just does not develop. There may be medical reasons for this, such as postnatal depression or challenges in attaching to a premature baby or the baby may be a result of rape or has a disability. While none of these may lead to immediate physical or emotional abuse or the neglect of the infant, they can be contributing factors.

Attachment in ECEC settings

The period from conception to the age of two is recognised as a crucial period for intervening early in the attachment process; however, as Balbernie (2015) reminds us, it is never too late to promote positive relationships. This is really important for those working in ECEC as children as young as a few months attend childminders or group care, yet there appear to be wide differences in ECEC pedagogy in relation to the care of babies and infants (Elfer and Page 2015). Given the policy imperatives for working households and the increased focus on the amount of free childcare families can have, this situation cannot continue. Infants and young children have the right to be cared for by people who understand the importance of attachment. They need to be nurtured in attachment-sensitive settings that work in partnership with parents and, where relevant, other professionals. ECEC also has a responsibility to provide opportunities for infants and young children to develop attachments to professionals and practitioners who are sensitive to their needs and who are able to see the world from their perspective, viewing them as active members of the setting.

The work of Bowlby (2007) and Gerhardt (2014) reminds us that babies and young children are particularly susceptible to emotional stress. Ongoing high arousal can cause increased levels of the stress hormone cortisol, which can impact on brain development and later behaviour. Where babies and young children are securely attached and have developed an attachment to a secondary carer in the setting, they are more able to manage the separation from their main caregivers. They are also generally more resilient, sociable and playful than their insecure peers. For those with insecure attachments, or where the transition and separation processes are not managed sensitively and there is an inconsistent secondary carer, there is a higher risk of the child being in a prolonged state of high arousal. This can impact negatively on their development and, as Gerhardt (2014, p.82) contends, 'A lot of the behaviour that worries us in later childhood, such as aggression, hyperactivity, obesity, depression and poor school performance, has already been shaped by children's experiences in babyhood'.

Siegel and Bryson (2011) have developed a framework for supporting parents with attachment that focuses on the '4 Ss' of attachment: 'seen', 'safe', soothed' and 'secure'. This framework has the potential to be used in ECEC to support policy, practice and training (based on Siegel and Bryson 2011):

Seen: This is closely aligned with mind-mindedness and mentalisation. It is about a deeper engagement with the child, seeing infants and children with empathy, and trying to understand what the child's behaviour is showing about how they experience the world. The practitioner also needs to think about how they feel, what they think and why about different situations, to enable them to then think of the situation through the eyes of others.

Safe: Avoiding actions and responses that have the potential to frighten or hurt a child.

Soothed: Helping children manage difficult emotions and situations. Young children need to learn to self-regulate and, for some, this is more difficult than for others, depending on their internal view of the world.

Secure: Enabling children to develop an internalised sense of wellbeing and worth, through nurturing, safe environments from which they experience the world.

Exercise: Promoting attachment in ECEC

- Why is understanding attachment important in ECEC?
- Think about the '4 Ss' of attachment. Write a list for each one about how they are they promoted in your workplace or placement.
- Many young children spend large amounts of their Early Years in ECEC settings. How does your setting or placement 'claim' the child so that they feel part of the community?
- What role do you think the Key Person for a child has in promoting attachment? What happens when they are not there?
- How does your workplace or placement support parents' understanding about attachment and how the setting focuses on this?

Practice point: The importance of understanding attachment theory

Those working in ECEC settings will not know, nor should they, all the details of a child's life or family circumstances. It is not their responsibility to assess or make judgements about the attachment of a child to their primary caregivers. Assessing insecure attachment is a skilled process that should be undertaken by a multi-professional team. Furthermore, practitioners, like parents, know that some days, children are happy just to go off and play, and other days they can be clingy for no apparent reason. Settings should provide safe and secure environments where children are seen and nurtured. Attachment theory should be applied to all transitions in the setting, whether group provision or homecare, to meet the specific needs of individual children.

In situations where there is a welfare concern or maltreatment has occurred, the importance of high-quality observations to support the wider assessment process is vital. As Doyle (2014, p.240) states, 'Early Years Workers are experts in the day to day understanding of young children'. They have so much to contribute to any assessment process being completed (see Chapter 7).

Chapter summary

This chapter has introduced the importance of understanding the differing perspectives about attachment for practice in ECEC. Practitioners need to understand the complexities of this vital process in an infant's development, and never make assumptions. Assessing attachment is a complex process that requires a multi-professional approach. While insecure attachment does not mean that an infant or child will experience physical or emotional abuse and neglect, it can be a contributing factor.

However, we know that securely attached infants and children are more likely to have the protective factors that support resilience, the capacity to manage adversity, develop positive relationships and be empathetic to others. With infants from a few months old being cared for by childminders and in group care, it is imperative that ECEC has attuned practitioners working within it and the environments are attachment-aware.

Key learning

- From birth, babies need to feel safe and secure, receiving nurturing, sensitive care from their primary caregivers.
- A baby's first attachment is usually with their mother.
- Attachment processes are initially biologically driven, but the nature of the attachment is experience-dependent.
- The four basic attachment behaviours are proximity seeking, secure base effect, safe haven and separation protest. These can be seen across all cultures.
- There are two main categories of attachment: 'secure' and 'insecure'. About 60 per cent of the population is securely attached and 40 per cent insecurely.
- Insecure attachment has been further categorised, and research suggests disorganised attachment is most prevalent in child maltreatment.
- The importance of parents and primary caregivers providing a *secure base* and developing 'mind-mindfulness' is vitally important in developing secure attachment.
- Infants can form attachments with a range of caregivers.
- Through the attachment process, the infant develops an Integral Working Model that is not fixed.
- Insecure attachment does not necessarily lead to child maltreatment. Research indicates that about 40 per cent of the population is insecurely attached.
- ECEC has a vital role for *all* children, not just those who have experienced maltreatment in providing attachment-aware environments and attuned practitioners.

Useful resources

For advice and guidance

Center on the Developing Child at Harvard University, http://developingchild.harvard.edu

Allan Schore is a clinical scientist at the University of California. His research has focused on the integration of psychological and biological models of emotional and social development across the lifespan. He has produced several films on attachment that will support your learning. The film of his lecture in Oslo in 2014 is particularly useful: Schore, A. (2014b) *Neuroscience and Attachment Theory. The Right Brain and Its Importance in the First Years.* Available at www.youtube.com/watch?v=KW-S4cyEFCc&t=1645s

Sir Richard Bowlby, son of the late John Bowlby, has produced a number of short films exploring the importance of attachment theory in early years practice: see www.youtube.com/playlist?list=PL1BA50B1137D450D8

Further reading

Cairns, K. and Cairns B. (2016) *Attachment, Resilience and Trauma.* London: British Association for Adoption and Fostering (BAAF). Invaluable insights into caring for children who have experienced trauma.

Elfer, P., Goldsmeid, E. and Selleck, D. (2012) *Key Persons in the Early Years: Building Relationships for Quality Provision in Early Years Settings and Primary Schools* (2nd edn). Abingdon: Routledge. The Key Person approach is evident in many ECEC settings. This book considers the role and its challenges as well as providing practical advice.

O'Connor, A. (2013) *Early Years: Supporting Change through Attachment and Resilience.* Abingdon: Routledge. One of the characteristics of Early Childhood is the numerous transitions infants and young children make. This book explores this area in detail, considers good practice and provides practice guidance.

Perry, B. and Szalavitz, M. (2017) *The Boy Who Was Raised by a Dog* (3rd edn). New York: Basic Books. This latest edition of this renowned book provides case study insights into the impact of trauma on children's lives.

Wilkins, D., Shemmings, D. and Shemmings, Y. (2015) *A–Z of Attachment*. London: Palgrave. This is an extremely useful extended glossary of attachment concepts.

Chapter 5

The Impact of Child Abuse and Adverse Childhood Experiences

Chapter objectives

By the end of this chapter you will be able to:
- Explain the consequences of Adverse Childhood Experiences (ACEs) on the holistic development of young children
- Describe basic brain development and the impact of neglect on the brain's architecture
- Discuss the short-, medium- and long-term impact of early traumatic experiences
- Appreciate the vital role of ECEC in the early detection, intervention and development of resilience in young children.

Introduction

An infant or young child who is being abused or where abuse is suspected will not only need protection from harm, but also support to understand what has happened to them. There are no easy solutions, and children will respond differently depending on a whole range of factors, including the nature of the abuse, how long it lasted, the age it started and if any support was provided. Furthermore, the actual investigation involving medicals and, depending on the age of the child, interviews, can further traumatise the child. They may also have been removed from their immediate family to another family member or into the care of the local authority. This disrupts normal routines and widens the number of adults they have to engage with. All of this can lead to distress, uncertainty and confusion for the child, and they may even blame themselves for what has happened.

It is important to reinforce again that not all child abuse is detected, and that the majority of children experiencing what are now more widely termed 'Adverse Childhood Experiences' (ACEs) remain living with their families. The focus of this chapter is to enable those studying Early Childhood and working in ECEC to understand the complex lives of some infants and young children. It considers how early experiences of neglect and child abuse impact on the brain and emotional development, health and wellbeing, learning and later life outcomes. There is also a focus on the role of ECEC in supporting improved outcomes for children.

Adverse childhood experiences

The term ACEs is now commonly used to refer to the range of potentially traumatic or toxic experiences encountered by children that cause chronic stress and can impact on their short-, medium- and long-term development. The influential ACE study in North America found an association between ACEs and health and social problems as an adult (Felitti *et al.* 1998). Ten types of ACEs were identified that embrace personal experiences of physical, emotional and sexual abuse, emotional and physical neglect and environment factors. These include domestic violence, substance misuse (alcohol and drugs), mental illness, parental separation and/or divorce and a family member in prison. In other words, ACEs include factors where the child is directly harmed through maltreatment and/or by living in stressful environments. The original study found that substantial numbers of children experience at least one ACE. For those who had multiple adverse experiences, the range of health, social and emotional problems experienced over the life course increased substantially. These include alcoholism, depression, heart disease and diabetes.

These findings have been reinforced by studies in the UK (Bellis *et al.* 2014; Ford *et al.* 2016; Public Health Wales 2015; Sabates and Dex 2012). In Wales, for example, ACE research has influenced investment in the Early Years and the *Well-being of Future Generations (Wales) Act 2015* (Welsh Government 2015). In Scotland, a scoping of policy and procedures found that ACE research was already influencing decision-making. Furthermore, the Scottish Government is investing in Early Years to improve life outcomes (Couper and Mackie 2016), and Glasgow has developed an ACE tracker to provide more targeted support (Scottish Government 2017). A further study across three local authority areas in England concluded that policy and procedures aimed at reducing ACEs would '...not only lessen the prevalence of health-harming behaviours and prevent unintended teenage pregnancy, but also prevent violent behaviour, thus helping to break the cycle of adversity that families can become trapped into' (Ford *et al.* 2016, p.1).

CASE STUDY: STEFAN AND PETRA

Stefan, aged three, and Petra, aged four, have been in the care of the local authority for nine months and are living with foster carers. They were not known to the authorities before this. The long-term plan is to place both children for adoption rather than return to them to the care of their parents or wider family members.

They were removed from their parents following a child abuse investigation. The children were found to have severe bruising on their arms and legs, Petra had signs of previous broken bones and both were underweight, had teeth decay, thrush in their mouths and head lice. Both children were very withdrawn and had poor language development. Their parents were unemployed and both smoked, took drugs and were heavy drinkers. The family had lived in a sparsely furnished flat and the children had slept on a mattress on the floor. When they were received into care, the authorities found no food in the flat and the children had very few clothes or toys.

Exercise: Adverse experiences
- Make a list of the ACEs experienced by each child.
- Drawing on the information from Chapters 2–4, compile a list of what you think the impact may be on the behaviour and physical and emotional wellbeing of the children.

Practice point: The impact of adverse experiences
One of the real strengths of working in ECEC is the amount of contact practitioners have with infants and very young children over a prolonged period. Therefore, those working in Early Years should have a good understanding of the range of 'normal' behaviour and responses from children, and be able to sense when something does not feel 'right'. In this particular case study, there is very little detail provided about Stefan and Petra's experiences, highlighting that not all families facing challenges are known to Children's Services. However, a number of ACEs that the children have experienced can be identified. How these will affect each child's development and behaviour is not exactly known

and will depend on a range of factors, including how each child responds to intervention.

ACEs experienced by Stefan and Petra

- Physical abuse – the previous fractures could indicate previous untreated physical abuse
- Neglect indicated by their weight, physical health, lack of food and home environment
- Drug and alcohol misuse by the adults, who both smoked
- Potential emotional abuse
- Separation from parents.

Possible developmental and behavioural effects

- Normal healthy development may be impaired, including cognitive development, growth, eyesight and long-term dental health.
- Impaired emotional wellbeing, including low self-esteem, lack of confidence and mental health issues including depression and post-traumatic stress disorder (PTSD). The children may present as unhappy and sad. These poor self-images may continue throughout the life course, and may result in ongoing mental health issues, including self-harm and ritualised behaviour.
- Behaviour may be challenging and disruptive. The children may be aggressive, have temper tantrums or be withdrawn or a mixture of them all. They may not be able to understand consequences of their actions or make decisions, issues that can be lifelong.
- Sexualised behaviour towards themselves and others, including adults.
- Difficulty in making appropriate relationships.

Brain development and the impact of adverse experiences

This section focuses on the developing brain and how adverse life experiences including abuse can influence this. It is an area of increasing importance for all working in Early Childhood, as our knowledge of brain development has advanced exponentially. Neuroscience research into brain activity is providing powerful insights into the impact of an infant's earliest experiences on the architecture of the brain, how genes are turned on or not, and their subsequent development. With the increasing numbers of infants and young children using ECEC provision for longer periods of time, understanding brain development takes on a new importance.

At a minimum adults working in ECEC need a basic understanding of the brain's architecture and how it develops. They need to recognise the importance of research-informed practice and appreciate the significance of the very Early Years from conception to two years old (Wave Trust 2013). They also need to know about how attachment processes influence the developing brain and the role of 'serve and return' (Center on the Developing Child 2016) or the 'dance' (Hughes 2006), discussed in Chapter 4. Consequently, unresponsive or unpredictable adults or adverse environments can impede holistic development in the short, medium and long term.

While caution must be applied to applying research findings (Doyle and Timms 2014), the growing knowledge base from neuroscience and molecular biology is invaluable. This knowledge about the science of child development enhances understanding of the potential impact of ACEs, especially neglect on brain development, and the importance of promoting 'nurturing care and protection to improve developmental outcomes' (Britto *et al.* 2017, p.99).

There is some excellent practice in Early Years, yet, despite considerable investment by successive governments in England, the disadvantage gap is not reducing (Ofsted 2016). This reinforces the challenges presented by inter-generational societal issues that act as barriers to change, and confirms the importance of intervening in the 'very' Early Years period prior to infants and young children starting at an ECEC setting. However, more recent research into *epigenetics*, which focuses on the potential for the brain to adapt to environmental factors, promises exciting opportunities for practice in Early Childhood, as does the increasing knowledge about the factors that promote resilience in young children. ECEC has the potential to make a real difference, not only to the long-term social and emotional development of infants and young children, but also to their early learning and future educational achievements (see Chapter 8).

How the brain develops

Brain development is dynamic, starting at conception and continuing across the life course. The ongoing architecture of the brain is impacted on by the quality of the foundations laid down in the first few years of life. The following discussion provides a brief insight into the development and composition of the brain. (The Center on the Developing Child at Harvard University has some short films that bring this alive – see 'Useful resources' at the end of this chapter.)

The development of the brain is often likened to building a house, with a 'critical' or 'sensitive' period in the process of building the infrastructure to ensure the house is built properly (National Scientific Council on the Developing Child 2007). The infant is born with the brain's structure in place, and it is the experiences thereafter that influence how it develops (Center on the Developing Child 2016; Conkbayir 2017; Doyle and Timms 2014; Oates, Karmiloff-Smith and Johnson 2012).

There are three main parts to the brain:

Brain stem: This is the oldest part of the brain and connects the brain to the spinal cord. It controls, for example, breathing, body temperature, heart rate and blood pressure.

Cerebellum: This is situated at the rear of the brain and controls, for example, balance and coordination.

Cerebrum: This is the largest part of the brain and is responsible for higher functions such as memory, thinking and feeling. The outer surface of the cerebrum is called the cerebral cortex. This gives the brain its rippled appearance and enables the brain to have a larger surface area.

Another important area of the brain is the *hippocampus,* which looks like a seahorse. It is situated inside the brain and has important functions for memory and controls the release of stress hormones including cortisol. Understanding the impact of stress hormones, discussed later in this chapter, is important for those working with infants and young children, especially in relation to those experiencing abuse or living in adverse environments.

The brain is composed of two main types of cells, *neurons* and *glial.* Each neuron comprises three main parts:

Cell body: This contains the nucleus, which is circular in shape.

Axon: This looks like roots of a tree and sends out messages to other neurons and is covered in myelin, a fatty sheath that enhances communication between the neurons.

Dendrites: This is the part of the neuron that receives messages from other neurons.

Neurons communicate with each other by a small electrical charge through the spaces between the *axon* called the *synapse*. For this to happen, infants and young children '...need stimulation and consistent experiences to develop firm communications between neurons and synapses' (Doyle and Timms 2014, p.37). Glial cells have a number of important supporting functions to neurons. One of their roles is to produce *myelin* on the *axon* that enables the quicker transmission of information.

A baby is born with about 100 billion neurons, and 250,000 of these are produced within the first four months of pregnancy. In the first few years of life more than a million new neuron connections are made every second, and by the age of two, the brain is 80 per cent of its adult size. It has almost twice as many connections as it needs in adulthood, and research suggests that childhood and adolescence experiences influence the connections kept or those discarded through a process known as *pruning*. This enables the most important connections to be strengthened and improves their efficiency (Center on the Developing Child 2016; Conkbayir 2017; Doyle and Timms 2014; Oates *et al.* 2012).

The brain also has amazing skill capacity that requires a working memory, mental flexibility and self-control known as *executive function and self-regulation*. Executive function is developed through relationships with adults and the environments that young children interact with. The attachment processes discussed in the previous chapter have an important role here. For infants and young children who are abused or living in adverse environments, the development of their executive function and abilities to self-regulate can be impaired. However, as Doyle and Timms (2014, p.39) point out, the brain is not a static system – it is '...a dynamic neutral system and has the ability to adapt and change in response to inputs such as novel experiences or injuries'.

Consequently, the brain has the capacity to change over the life course and make new connections. This ability is referred to as brain *plasticity* or *neuroplasticity*, and intervention can make a positive difference for infants and young children who have faced adversity. This, alongside increasing knowledge about epigenetics, as discussed earlier, provides renewed optimism that intervention, especially through high-quality ECEC, can improve longer-term outcomes. However, it is important to note that for some children who have experienced neglect, especially prolonged neglect and emotional abuse, where brain development has been severely impeded change is difficult, and the cognitive and emotional consequences are lifelong (Doyle and Timms 2014).

Exercise: Executive function and self-regulation
The Center on the Developing Child (2017b) suggests that executive function and self-regulation can be supported by adults through:
- Routines
- Modelling social behaviour
- Creating and supporting reliable relationships
- Providing opportunism for creative play
- Engagement with others
- Managing stress
- Exercise.
- How are each of these addressed in your workplace or placement setting?

Reflection point
The development of the brain is complex, and research clearly indicates that the earliest years are vital for developing the brain architecture and how the brain adapts during the life course. Consider what you have learned about brain development and ACEs.

Write yourself three lists, identifying:

- What you think are the optimal conditions for brain development from conception.
- What factors you think act as barriers to brain development.
- What support should be provided to new parents or caregivers during pregnancy and in the Early Years to promote their understanding of brain development.

Diet during pregnancy is important to support the developing baby. Poor nutrition, smoking, substance misuse, maternal depression, socioeconomic status and living in stressful environments, including domestic violence, can all impact on the brain's development. They can also lead to health issues in the short, medium and long term for the unborn child (British Medical Association Board of Science 2013; Holmes 2017; Marmot 2010).

Research has found that some parents, predominantly mothers, who neglect their children have challenges with negotiating and problem-solving. They may be limited in their own emotional language and have medical and psychological issues, such as depression. They may also gravitate to a partner who abuses them and engages in substance misuse. Environmental factors such as poverty, unemployment and poor housing can also be present (British Medical Association Board of Science 2013; Doyle and Timms 2014).

CASE STUDY: LUCAS

Lucas is two years old and has just started to attend nursery for 15 hours per week. The health visitor has been concerned about the relationship between Lucas and his mother, and her ability to meet his developing needs as well as manage their home. Since he has started at the nursery there have been concerns that it is hard to engage him in activities, he has a limited vocabulary and difficulty speaking, and often sits and rocks. He is often hungry and has not always been washed or had his hair combed.

His mother, Lucy, is 19 and is a lone parent and entered the care system at the age of ten. She had several foster homes before being placed in a residential home. She has a police record for theft and grievous bodily harm against another resident at the residential home.

She shows no interest in knowing what her son is doing at nursery, and tends to shout at him to 'get a move on' when she collects him. She is often late for the start of the session and collecting him, and sometimes smells of alcohol.

Exercise: Intervening early
- Make a list of all the issues that are concerning you in this case study.
- Make a list of what actions you think the setting should take.
- What early learning opportunities would promote Lucas' holistic development?

Early intervention with families can make a real difference, although it is important to realise that there are no quick remedies; rather, families need ongoing support. In this case study, there are indicators that Lucas' development and relationship with his mother are problematic and that Lucy is struggling with the demands of parenting. Her own background may contribute to her ability to parent and respond appropriately to his needs. As well as following procedures for safeguarding, the setting can focus on ensuring he has a consistent adult (Key Person) and another member of staff who will take responsibility if his Key Person is unavailable. Planning needs to focus on providing opportunities for Lucas that promote all aspects of his development, including activities that are rich in language and creativity and that offer plentiful opportunities to build his confidence and self-efficacy.

Toxic stress

One of the consequences of ACEs for children being maltreated or living in adverse environments is that their stress hormones are raised. This can alter the brain's architecture and the function of other organs, leading to lifelong health issues. These include obesity, diabetes and heart disease as well as depression, substance misuse and self-harming as well as low education attainment and anti-social behaviour (Center on the Developing Child 2016). Furthermore, the unborn baby may be affected by the stress experienced by some mothers during pregnancy, which can lead to raised stress levels, early birth and low birth weight (Doyle and Timms 2014).

Reflection point

Think about the last time you experienced stress:

- What was the occasion?
- How did you feel?
- How did your body respond?
- What did you do to self-regulate?
- What do you think the impact on your wellbeing would be if you continually faced high levels of stress?

It is important to appreciate that not all stress is bad: it is a natural response to certain situations. Doyle and Timms (2014, pp.40–41) provide a useful overview of what happens to the body in what is known as a 'fight or flight' response to stress.

Stress releases adrenaline, which increases the heart rate, blood pressure and breathing rate. Simultaneously, glucose is produced by the kidneys and blood containing the glucose and oxygen travels to the brain and main muscles.

The physiological response to stress is managed through three hormone system – the adrenocorticotropic, vasopressin and thyroxine systems. At times of stress, the adrenocorticotropic system secretes corticosteroids, which include cortisol and aldosterone. Prolonged high levels of cortisol can have a negative impact on the body and have been found in high levels in children who are abused, even into adulthood.

For infants and young children attending ECEC, being separated from their primary carers is stressful. For children who are abused and/or are living in adverse environments, high levels of stress are normal. Attending ECEC can actually add further levels of stress. Understanding the physical and physiological impact on their behaviour and development, as well as understanding why their primary caregivers may respond in the way they do, is essential. Providing nurturing environments that positively address social and emotional development alongside nutritional needs is imperative. Settings with a well-trained and stable workforce can provide opportunities for young children to develop resilient characteristics that support the building blocks to manage adversity and strengthen the core skills required across the life course.

The importance of resilience

One of the most important things to remember is that experiencing abuse or living in adverse environments is responded to differently by different children – and some grow stronger from the experiences (Joslyn 2016). There has been considerable research into the factors that make some children manage the adversity they experience more effectively than others. The main finding is that those children who have developed more resilience have:

...at least one stable and responsive relationship with a parent, caregiver or other adult. These relationships that provide the support, scaffolding and protection that both buffer children from developmental disruptions and help build key capabilities. (Center on the Developing Child 2016, p.16)

It is believed that resilience supports the development of the relevant skills to manage the challenges they face. At an individual level, resilience builds on the attributes and child's attitude to developing skills and competencies. One of the important lessons I learned as a social worker was from a grandmother applying for guardianship of her grandchild. His mother was an alcoholic and lived a chaotic lifestyle and was unable to meet his developmental needs. The grandmother talked about the importance of identifying his skill in something and giving him every opportunity to develop it, and if he chose not to pursue that skill, to find another one. The message was clear: she saw her job and that of his extended family as building his confidence and skills so that he had the foundation to manage his challenging relationship with his mother.

Developing a good sense of self, self-regulation and emotional literacy, as well as positive relationships with adults other than their main caregivers, are all areas that can be influenced by attending high-quality ECEC (see Chapter 8).

Chapter summary

This chapter has specifically focused on how the full range of ACEs can influence how the brain develops. For some children, this can have a lifelong and intergenerational impact, especially in cases of severe neglect or when the child is subjected to highly stressful environments. Ongoing exposure to stressful situations results in the ongoing secretion of excessive hormones, especially cortisone. Therefore, early detection and intervention is crucial, alongside sensitive nurturing and attuned ECEC environments that can support the development of resilience in infants and young children.

Key learning

- ACEs embrace individual experiences such as abuse and toxic stress as well as environmental experiences such as poverty and the 'toxic three' of mental health, domestic violence and substance misuse.
- Exposure to ACEs can start from conception, impacting on the brain's development, which can have lifelong and intergenerational consequences. These include the development of the brain's executive function and consequently the ability for the child to develop self-regulation.
- Children experiencing ACEs are more likely to succeed if they have at least one stable relationship that supports the development of resilience.
- Research into epigenetics has an important potential for ECEC in providing environments that can lead to improved developmental outcomes.
- ECEC has a vital role in early detection and intervention. It can also provide nurturing environments that promote and build on young children's attributes, enabling them to develop skills and competencies to manage adversity more effectively.

Useful resources

For advice and guidance
Center on the Developing Child at Harvard University, http://developingchild.harvard.edu/science. This website has short films and key concept papers on the development of the brain.

ACEs, www.cdc.gov/violenceprevention/acestudy/index.html. This website has links to all the original research and a range of resources.

Further reading

Center on the Developing Child at Harvard University (2016) *From Best Practice to Breakthrough Impacts: A Science Based Approach for Building a More Promising Future for Young Children and Families.* Available at http://developingchild.harvard.edu/wp-content/uploads/2016/05/From_Best_Practices_to_Breakthrough_Impacts-4.pdf. The Center on the Developing Child is an excellent source of contemporary research in Early Childhood. This report draws on research evidence and suggests ways in which children and their families can be supported.

Conkbayir, M. (2017) *Early Childhood and Neuroscience: Theory, Research and Implications for Practice.* London: Bloomsbury Academic. This text introduces those working in Early Childhood to the importance of understanding neuroscience, and how this knowledge and understanding can enhance practice and outcomes for young children.

Doyle, C. and Timms, C. (2014) *Child Neglect and Emotional Abuse: Understanding, Assessment and Response.* London: Sage. This book explores the complex nature of neglect and emotional abuse and working with vulnerable children. There is a really useful section on brain development.

Joslyn, E. (2016) *Resilience in Childhood: Perspectives, Promise and Practice.* London: Palgrave Macmillan. This book explores the complex area of resilience and how children can be supported in developing autonomy, become self-reliant and develop independence.

Chapter 6

Legislation, Policy and Procedures

Chapter objectives

By the end of this chapter you will be able to:
- Discuss the importance of child protection legislation, policies and procedures
- Understand the stages of a child abuse investigation and possible outcomes
- Explain your role in advocating for infants and young children
- Know how to refer concerns in relation to ECEC practice and safeguarding.

Introduction

The importance of protecting children from harm is enshrined in Article 19 of the 1989 UNCRC (UNICEF 1989). The Convention also recognises the importance of providing services for children who have faced maltreatment (Article 39). However, achieving both of these in a complex and diverse world is an aspiration, mainly because countries have differing perspectives on intervening in family life and what they view as justifiable physical chastisement or abuse.

In the UK the safeguarding of children is everyone's responsibility, and those working with children have a duty to follow safeguarding procedures and participate in assessments and any subsequent Child Protection Plans. While the welfare and best interests of children should be paramount at all times, the State only intervenes in family life when it has to. Furthermore, wherever possible, the focus of intervention is to enable the child to remain in their family and not to come into local authority care.

The focus of this chapter, therefore, is to introduce the legislation, policies and procedures that inform practice in ECEC. The chapter is divided into four sections: legislation and statutory guidance, levels of need and assessment processes, the child protection process, and policy and procedures in ECEC settings. Where relevant, the language of child protection legislation and procedures is explained and the variations in the different countries of the UK identified.

Legislation and statutory guidance

In each of the four nations of the UK, the legislative and subsequent statutory guidance and policy frameworks for child protection enable the State to intervene in family life. This occurs when there are concerns that the safety and wellbeing of children is falling short of what society deems acceptable. However, no family is the same – they are made up of complex relationships and different beliefs and practices for raising children. Therefore, making the decision to remove children from their family is a difficult and contentious issue, and is arguably one of the greatest responsibilities and power the State has. Court orders to remove children should only be made if it is deemed a better alternative for the child than remaining in the family (Herring 2017; Holt 2014). This situation has been further reinforced by the *Human*

Rights Act 1998, which strengthens the family's right to privacy. Consequently, the decision-making processes that lead to a child being removed from their family must reflect the involvement of the family, and that the child's rights and welfare have been paramount (Herring 2017).

Legislation, which is also referred to as Acts of Parliament or statutes, is the primary source of law in the UK. Some statutes are for the whole of the country and others are specific to individual nations. The statutory guidance provides the legal duties that local authorities need to act on using non-legal language. Local authorities use these duties to develop local policy and procedures that comply with national legislation and statutory guidance. This then forms the basis for ECEC settings to develop their own safeguarding policy and procedures that govern practice in the setting.

In relation to child protection, England and Wales have the same law, but the statutory guidance and procedures implementing the legislative requirements are different. The *Children Act 1989* is the core legislation but has had some sections amended and extended by subsequent legislation, including the *Adoption and Children Act 2002*, *Children Act 2004* and *Children and Social Work Act 2017*. Scotland has different legislation – the *Children (Scotland) Act 1995*, passed by the Scottish Parliament – as does Northern Ireland, with the Northern Ireland Executive Government being responsible for *The Children (Northern Ireland) Order 1996*.

All of the statutes have two primary areas of concern:

- *Children and young people deemed to be 'in need':* The local authority must provide services to meet the holistic needs of children who have physical and/or learning disabilities and health issues, as well as those who may be at risk of harm. In Scotland, 'in need' also embraces other children in the family who may be affected by a disabled sibling. (The complexities of defining need and the threshold for services are considered further in the next section.)

- *Children and young people at risk of or who have experienced significant harm:* Here the focus is on the law that addresses child protection procedures taking emergency action and making court orders. This can be either a full Care Order, where the children become 'looked after' by the local authority, which has the ultimate decision-making responsibilities for the child, or a Supervision Order. A Supervision Order means that the child remains at home but the local authority has a statutory role 'to advise, assist and befriend the child' (Holt 2014, p.3).

Practice point: Child protection and safeguarding

In England, there is a distinction between child protection legislation, which is key to the *Children Act 1989* and the safeguarding of children. The *Children Act 2004* defines safeguarding as promoting the wellbeing of children (Carr and Goosey 2017).

As previously discussed, while the *Children Act 1989*, *Children (Scotland) Act 1995* and *The Children (Northern Ireland) Order 1996* are the primary legal frameworks for the different countries of the UK, amendments have been made to improve, clarify or extend specific areas of the law. For example, only parents who were married had joint parental responsibility under the *Children Act 1989* for England and Wales. Even if the birth father was named on the birth certificate, if they were not married he did not, in law, have parental responsibility for his children, although he was seen as having financial responsibility. This was changed by the *Adoption and Children Act 2002*, but responsibility is still not automatic for the father if he is not married to the child's mother, although there are a range of options including being present at the registration of the birth and a Parental Responsibility Agreement (Herring 2017). This situation is similar in both Scotland and Northern Ireland (GOV.UK 2017).

Reflection point

Parental responsibility is defined in the various statutes, and concerns the responsibilities of birth parents for their children. Practitioners do not always know about the legal complexities of this area.

- Were you aware of the issues surrounding parental responsibility?
- What do you think are the potential safeguarding issues in ECEC if the father does not have parental responsibility and is estranged from the children and their mother?
- What policies does your setting or placement setting have for the arrival and departure of the children?

Central to the three legislative frameworks is the belief that the child's welfare is of paramount importance and that the biological mother always has parental responsibility. Adoption is the only way this changes and, when an Adoption Order is granted, a new certificate is provided that replaces the original birth certificate. It names the adopters, or in stepparent adoptions, the birth and stepparent, as the legal parents.

Parental responsibility for the father is more complex. Therefore, knowing who has parental responsibility is important in ECEC, as are the names and contact details of those authorised to bring and collect the children from the setting. If the father does not have parental responsibility and is not named as a person who will collect his child/ren from the setting, they cannot be permitted to go with him.

Levels of need and assessment processes

All local authorities provide universal services to meet the needs of their local communities (see Table 6.1). However, some children and families require additional services, although not all families want to access these. Unless there are specific child welfare concerns that legally require intervention, the right of parents not to access services must be respected. This can be really challenging for professionals and practitioners who know the children and family will benefit from intervention. If services are provided, they can be for a limited period or be more targeted. More specialist services may also be required, for example, when child abuse has occurred. In England, Wales and Scotland, local procedures and protocols are available on the web pages of the local authority and the local safeguarding children board, and in Northern Ireland on the safeguarding board and local safeguarding panel websites (see the suggested websites at the end of this chapter).

Exercise: The importance of knowing your local policy and services

Each of the four nations and the local authorities within them vary in the services provided and in the names of services and assessment processes used. There are also national charities and more bespoke local charities providing services in local authorities, as well as other third-sector organisations.

- How much do you know about the relevant policy and resources in your area? Use the internet to find out:
  - What services the local authority provides for children and families in your area
  - What charities operate in your area
  - Whether there are any community groups.
- Investigate the local authority and local safeguarding children boards' websites for information about needs assessment, safeguarding and local protocols.
  - How do you think this knowledge will promote effective practice in work with children and their families?

Understanding the community in which you work really enables high-level engagement with children and their families. All professionals working in universal services have a responsibility to understand their role in identifying need, sharing information and contributing to assessment processes (DfE 2015a). Those working in ECEC have an important role in identifying families who may require early help, contributing to the assessment processes and child protection investigation, regardless of their role. Safeguarding procedures in a setting should clearly identify the pathways for sharing information within the setting as well as with external agencies (discussed later in this chapter).

Assessing the level of need is a complex and skilled process, and unmet need is not always apparent. When a child 'in need' has been identified, actually assessing the level of risk for the child is challenging and no case is the same. Agencies may also perceive risk differently, so for health professionals, risk may be around the health of the mother for the unborn baby, and in school, the risks may focus on a child's likely poor educational attainment. With increasing research about the impact of ACEs, as discussed in Chapter 5, the risk may be as a result of environmental factors. Consequently, good quality assessment processes in all aspects of children's social care are key in providing appropriate and timely assistance to children and their families. However, before an assessment is undertaken the level of need must be identified.

Levels of need

In work with children and families, four types of need have been identified, although the exact terminology used may be different in each local authority area (see Table 6.1). *Working Together to Safeguard Children* (DfE 2015a, p.13) has also identified a number of situations, applicable across the UK, where professionals need to be particularly vigilant. These are when the child or young person:

- Is disabled and has specific additional needs
- Has special educational needs
- Is a young carer

- Is showing signs of engaging in anti-social or criminal behaviour
- Is in a family circumstance that presents challenges for the child, such as substance misuse, adult mental health problems or domestic violence
- Has returned home to their family from care
- Is showing early signs of abuse and/or neglect.

Table 6.1: Levels of need

Universal	Health, education and other services meet the universal needs of the children and families in their area.
Early help	This may involve a situation that is easily resolved through signposting to a relevant service or the family may require an Early Help Assessment (EHA) to be completed (see Table 6.2). Short-term support is provided and the situation is resolved, or more targeted intervention is required.
Targeted	Following the EHA, a more specific need that requires a more targeted approach may be required. It is at this stage that social workers are more likely to become involved with families. 'Child in need' assessments may also be needed for children who have additional needs (see Table 6.2).
Specialist	This is where the risk factors are high and more intensive intervention is required. A child may be deemed as being at risk of significant harm or may have actually been abused.

Types of assessment

Currently, in England, there are three main types of assessment undertaken with children and families. These are the non-statutory EHA and two statutory assessments, child/ren 'in need' and child protection (see Table 6.2). If a child protection assessment is required, it must be conducted in a timely manner and reviewed regularly. It should gather relevant information about the child in the context of their family and community. This initial assessment considers what services are already involved with the family, the risks or potential risks and what intervention is needed to build on the family's strengths.

Table 6.2: Assessment of need

Early help	Local authorities are expected to provide a coordinated EHA to children and families as soon as problems become apparent. In England the *Working Together to Safeguard Children* documentation defines 'early help' as 'Providing support as the problem emerges at any point in a child's life from the foundation years through to teenage years' (DfE 2015a, p.12). An EHA is not statutory and is undertaken by a lead professional, who could be a family worker, health visitor, doctor or an Early Years Teacher, and it can only be undertaken if consent is given by the family. The EHA must be child-focused, involve the child and family throughout, and be focused on preventing an escalation of the situation.
Child 'in need'	This is a statutory assessment included in the respective statutes for children in the four nations of the UK. The assessment focuses on children who are seen to be 'in need' or who are at risk of harm or are actually suffering 'significant harm'. Each of the statutes defines what is meant by these terms, but broadly, children 'in need' includes those whose development or health may be impaired, for example, those who have a disability, who have additional educational needs, young carers and those displaying anti-social behaviour. The actual level of intervention may vary across the UK as thresholds are set at a local level. Local authorities must keep a formal record of all children with a disability in their area.

Child protection	In cases of significant harm, or if a referral has been made expressing concern about the welfare of a child, an assessment must be undertaken (see Figure 6.1). The assessment follows the respective legislation and statutory guidance for the four nations and the procedures at a local level. Each of the four nations has time frames for completing the specific parts of the assessment and for arranging the case conference. Significant harm definitions include ill treatment, impairment of health and/or development and witnessing the ill treatment of others. It includes children who experience or are likely to experience all types of abuse as well as living in environments that are harming their health and development. These include homes where substance misuse, mental health issues or domestic violence are present.

Assessment framework

An assessment framework is used to gather high-quality information about the needs and risk factors in a particular case and the intervention or action required. The child's needs are paramount and are central to the assessment process, and while different frameworks are used in the four nations, they all draw on ecological theory (see Bronfenbrenner 2005), and cover:

- The child's holistic development needs
- The parenting capacity of the parents to meet the child's needs
- Family and environmental factors and how these are impacting on the child.

All the frameworks require a multi-professional and inter-agency approach to promote information sharing with relevant information shared and discussed with the parents as appropriate (Calder, McKinnon and Sneddon 2012; DfE 2015a)

Child protection process

Regardless of the specific legislative framework, the general child protection procedures and stages of the investigation are the same in all the four nations of the UK (see Figure 6.1). While Children's Services take the lead role in the child protection process, this area of work requires different agencies working together, including health, education and the police (see Chapter 7). As mentioned at the start of this chapter, all local authorities in the UK have a safeguarding board that has overall responsibility for the policies, and in England, the local children safeguarding board also has responsibility for motoring and evaluation as well as training and undertaking SCRs. These are extremely detailed reviews that take place when a child dies or has been seriously harmed or there is concern about how agencies have worked together (DfE 2015a). In Scotland they are called *significant case reviews*, in Wales *case management reviews* and in Northern Ireland *child practice reviews* (NSPCC 2017c).

Practice point: Keeping up to date

Policy and legislation continually change, and so keeping up to date is a vital role of professional development. At the time of preparing this book, the *Children and Social Work Act 2017* in England became law. This will bring with it changes to local children safeguarding boards, *Working Together* processes and the current *Section 8* inquiries.

Practice point: Decision-making stages and possible outcomes

Child protection cases and decision-making processes are complex and confidential, and it can be difficult for practitioners, who may have referred concerns, to see the child remaining at home. It is therefore important that all those working in ECEC understand the decision-making stages and possible outcomes. The investigation may find that no further action is required or that the child/ren should:

- Be received into the care of the local authority
- Remain at home with their family
- Go and live with other family members (known as kinship care).

Furthermore, different decisions may be made about siblings in the same family as all children are assessed individually, which may mean different outcomes for each child. It is also really important to recognise a family's confidentiality. Information needs to be shared on a need-to-know basis rather than to all who work in the setting.

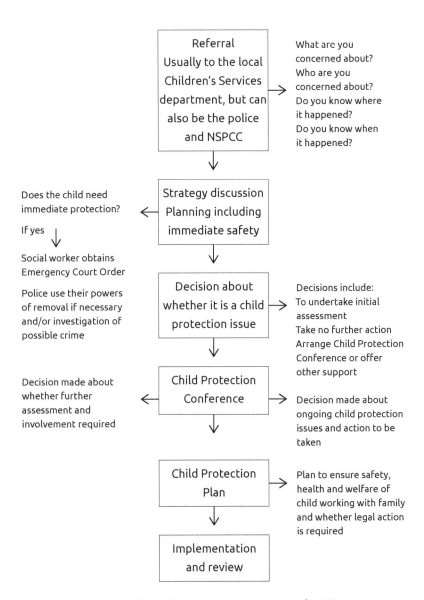

Figure 6.1: Overview of child protection processes in the UK

Referrals

A referral can be made by an agency or by anyone who has a child protection concern, including family members, neighbours or friends. The referral may also be in response to the EHA that has raised concerns about the child/ren being at risk of significant harm. At the point of referral, information about the exact concerns are required. These include:

- Who the concerns are about
- When the event was meant to have occurred
- What is meant to have happened
- What the factors are that are causing concern
- Who is suspected to be the perpetrator.

It is not always possible to get all the answers, and decisions have to be made with the safety of the child at the fore. The decisions include:

- Is immediate action required?
- Is it actually a child protection concern or is the referral malicious?
- Do the next stages of the protection procedures need to be activated?

The nature of the referral will also dictate whether the initial assessment needs to be conducted jointly with the police, for example, if there is an immediate danger to the child/ren or a crime has been committed.

If referrals are made to the police and NSPCC, they are usually referred directly to the team responsible for investigations in the local authority. More recently, Multi-Agency Safeguarding Hubs (MASH) have been established in local authorities, bringing together organisations and professionals in one team to respond to safeguarding referrals.

CHILD PROTECTION IN THE EARLY YEARS

Practice point: NSPCC and police powers in child protection

As well as the local authority, the NSPCC has specific powers that stem from its long history of working in child protection. The NSPCC is described in legislation as one of the 'authorised persons' in England, Wales and Northern Ireland. This gives it the statutory power to apply for court orders in child protection cases. However, in practice, it is more active in some local authorities than others, and usually passes any referrals directly to the local authority (Children Act 1989; NSPCC 2017d).

The police have powers to remove children in immediate danger where there is no time to apply for the relevant Emergency Protection Order. This order lasts for up to 72 hours in Northern Ireland, England and Wales, and 24 hours in Scotland. Usually, the police will undertake a joint investigation with social workers. Although the safety of the child is paramount, the police focus is on gathering evidence for possible prosecution.

Exercise: Child protection procedures

Given that the translation of legislation and statutory guidance varies across the four nations of the UK and across local authorities, it is important that you understand the procedures in your area both for child protection and any specific guidance for the Early Years sector.

- All local authorities have information about their child protection procedures on the internet. Research your local authority to find out:
  - What the referral procedures are
  - Whether there is a MASH.

- If yes:
  - What are the agencies involved?
  - What groups do they cover?
  - What is the specific child protection guidance for ECEC settings?

Initial assessment

The initial assessment is undertaken by a qualified social worker. It is an information-gathering process that needs to gain reliable information from those who know the child and family. If this initial brief assessment finds concerns about significant harm, a meeting between key professionals takes place to plan the action to be taken. At this point there are four main decisions that can be made:

- No further action.
- The situation does not warrant a full assessment, but the parents are offered assistance with specific issues, if they choose to accept it.
- Full investigation and assessment.
- Emergency action, a Court Order applied for and then a full investigation and assessment undertaken. At any point during the full investigation, an Emergency Protection Order may be applied for if the situation changes.

Emergency action

An *Emergency Protection Order* in England Wales and Northern Ireland is applied for from the court and in Scotland a *Child Protection Order* from the Sheriff. This is obviously a serious step to take, and the making of the order needs to be seen to be in the child's best interests as delay may lead to harm. The child is either removed to a place of safety or is already in a place of safety such as a hospital. The parents or caregivers are then prevented by law from removing the child. Alternatively, the child can remain at home and an *Exclusion Order* be made, excluding a named person from the home.

Full assessment

This needs to be a thorough, well-documented process that is child-centred and establishes the facts about the concerns being expressed, as well as the parent's willingness to work with professionals and agencies. It is a multi-professional assessment that uses the relevant assessment framework to assess the holistic needs of the child. It may therefore also involve a medical examination that can provide evidence for both the care proceedings (civil case) or criminal proceedings if a criminal offence has occurred.

Parents and the child, depending on the child's age, need to be active partners in the assessment process. However, the investigation and assessment processes are difficult and challenging for parents. This leads to some being abusive or refusing to cooperate with the assessment. In these difficult situations, or where there is no evidence to apply for an Emergency Protection Order but there are concerns about the child safety, a *Child Assessment Order* can be applied for from the court.

The next stage depends on the outcome of the assessment, and the child may be viewed as being 'in need' rather than in danger of being harmed. Work is then undertaken with the family to accept and engage with relevant professionals to address the issues the family is experiencing. Other cases proceed to the next stage, the Child Protection Conference.

Child Protection Conference

Following the initial assessment, a Child Protection Conference may be called to plan the next steps to ensure the safety of the child. It is a crucial part of the child protection process, and there may be subsequent conferences until the child is no longer deemed to be at risk of harm or a Care Order has been made and they are no longer living with their family. The conference should have an independent chair and the main purpose is to discuss and analyse the information presented and to develop a plan with timescales. It considers background information about the family, the assessment outcomes and findings from any other assessments that have been undertaken (Carr and Goosey 2017).

After all the information has been discussed and analysed, the conference chair leads all the professionals involved to make a decision about whether the child has been or is at risk of significant harm under the categories of physical, emotional or sexual abuse or neglect. A decision is made about whether a Child Protection Plan needs to be made or, in Wales, Scotland and Northern Ireland, whether the child's name goes on to the Child Protection Register (this register no longer exists in England; see Holt 2014). In some cases where the child is still living at home and information emerges at the conference that indicates that the child is at significant risk, action needs to be taken to ensure their immediate safety. In these situations, an Emergency Protection Order, or a Child Protection Order in Scotland, is applied for.

The conference brings together professionals involved alongside the relevant family members, and the child, depending on their age, is invited to attend. If they choose to attend they must be supported through the process. If they decide not to, any comments they have should be presented on their behalf. Parents can take someone to support them, although they cannot usually speak unless one or both parents has a disability. Parents can be excluded for a number of reasons, however, including if there is a risk of violence, mental health issues and attending under the influence of drugs or alcohol. In cases where the parents are estranged, especially if there is domestic violence, the parents can be invited to attend separately. Reports are written for the conference and the assessment report should be shared with the parents a few days before so they have time to absorb the information. This should enable them to actually contribute to the conference and challenge any inaccuracies (Holt 2014). The conference chair will meet with the parents prior to the conference starting, to 'ensure they understand the purpose and process' (DfE 2015a, p.43).

It is important that the professionals who attend the conference are involved with the child and family and are able to make a direct contribution to the discussion and decision-making process. The social worker always attends the conference as well as representatives from health, education and the police. The local authority legal department may also be present. In reality, conferences can be large and daunting for all attending, and especially for the family. However, the conference makes significant decisions that impact on the short-, medium- and long-term outcomes for children and families, and therefore requires careful management by the conference chair.

There are specific timescales in place for the different stages of the child protection process. A Child Protection Conference must be arranged in a timely manner that reflects the urgency of the specific circumstances of the case. In England. Wales and Northern Ireland, this is within 15 days of the initial strategy meeting, and in Scotland, 21 days from the initial referral (DfE 2015a; NSPCC 2017a). These timescales can be very challenging, and actually contacting the relevant professionals and gathering information can be difficult for the social worker undertaking the assessment.

Child Protection Plan

The recommendations of the Child Protection Conference form the basis for the Child Protection Plan. This process and the purpose of the plan are similar across the different nations of the UK. The plan aims to ensure the child's safety and promote their development and health. It must also support the family to safeguard the child and meet their needs (Carr and Goosey 2017; DfE 2015a; NSPCC 2017b). The plan has to set out how the child's welfare will be managed, who has responsibility for what actions, the support to be offered to the family and the changes needed to reduce risk. A more detailed assessment may be required to gain an in-depth understanding of the child's development needs and the support required to meet them.

A core group is established to ensure the plan is translated into practice. This group is jointly responsible for implementing, monitoring and adapting the plan. It comprises a small number of people with the social worker as the lead professional coordinating the plan and ensuring it is being implemented. In Scotland, the group liaises with the child's named person (Scottish Government 2017). The parents and/or carers are part of the group and, where appropriate, the child and other relevant professionals working with the family, for example, the health visitor, Early Years Teacher or a family worker. This group of professionals and practitioners is referred to as the Team Around the Family (TAF) (see Chapter 7).

The Child Protection Plan is reviewed in the first three months and then every six months to ascertain whether it is still required. The plan will cease if the child is no longer assessed as being at risk of harm, has died, reached the age of 18 or has permanently left the UK. If the family moves area to a new local authority, a Child Protection Conference has to take place within 15 days and the Child Protection Plan in the original local authority ceases (DfE 2015a). If the child's name is on a Child Protection Register (but not in England) it is removed when a plan is no longer required. However, in some cases, the child remains at risk of significant harm and the decision is made to apply for a Court Order.

Care proceedings

The process to obtain a Court Order can be activated at any point in the child protection process and can involve an application for a full Care Order or a Supervision Order. A Care Order gives the local authority the power to remove the child from their home. The processes are complex and decision-making starts from the principle that no order should be made. For a Court Order to be made, the thresholds laid out in the statutes for the four nations of the UK need to be met. Therefore care proceedings should not be entered into lightly; they are complex and subject to case law. Case law emerges from previous court cases and further defines how the law should be interpreted (Carr and Goosey 2017; Herring 2017; Holt 2014).

The local authority also needs to produce a Care Plan for the child that evidences how the child's needs will be met. This plan may work towards the child returning to live with their family or another family member, or state that they will live with foster carers in the short, medium or long term, or be placed for adoption.

Information sharing

Sharing information during child protection processes is required by law. Information provided should be factual, relevant and avoid subjectivity. However, professionals and practitioners are concerned that they will be in breach of data protection legislation and people's human rights. In order to clarify and support practitioners with their work, the English Government published *Information Sharing: Advice for Practitioners Providing Safeguarding Services to Children, Young People, Parents and Carers* (DfE 2015c). This guidance clarified that the overarching factor when deciding to share information is whether it will help '...safeguard and protect a child' (DfE 2015c, p.8). They also provided the 'golden rules', shown in Table 6.3, to support practitioners. These are applicable across the whole of the UK.

Table 6.3: The seven golden rules to sharing information

---

1. Remember that the *Data Protection Act 1998* and human rights law are not barriers to justified information sharing, but provide a framework to ensure that personal information about living individuals is shared appropriately.

---

2. Be open and honest with the individual (and/or their family where appropriate) from the outset about why, what, how and with whom information will, or could be, shared, and seek their agreement, unless it is unsafe or inappropriate to do so.

---

3. Seek advice from other practitioners if you are in any doubt about sharing the information concerned, without disclosing the identity of the individual where possible.

4. Share with informed consent where appropriate and, where possible, respect the wishes of those who do not consent to share confidential information. You may still share information without consent if, in your judgement, there is good reason to do so, such as where safety may be at risk. You will need to base your judgement on the facts of the case. When you are sharing or requesting personal information from someone, be certain of the basis upon which you are doing so. Where you have consent, be mindful that an individual might not expect information to be shared.

5. Consider safety and wellbeing. Base your information-sharing decisions on considerations of the safety and wellbeing of the individual and others who may be affected by their actions.

6. Necessary, proportionate, relevant, adequate, accurate, timely and secure: Ensure that the information you share is necessary for the purpose for which you are sharing it, is shared only with those individuals who need to have it, is accurate and up-to-date, is shared in a timely fashion, and is shared securely (see below).

7. Keep a record of your decision and the reasons for it –whether it is to share information or not. If you decide to share, then record what you have shared, with whom and for what purpose.

Source: DfE (2015c, p.4)

Policy and procedures in ECEC settings

As highlighted earlier in this chapter, each country of the UK has specific statutory guidance for child protection, including how agencies should work together. The principles underpinning the policies and procedures have synergy across the four nations. All providers of ECEC need a clear policy on safeguarding children, the safe recruitment of staff and what adults working in the setting should do if they are concerned about practice or a member of staff.

Safeguarding children

All staff should be aware of the procedures and understand the difference between child protection procedures (*Children Act 1989*) and the wider remit of safeguarding children through promoting their wellbeing (*Children Act 2004*). Staff also require ongoing training to ensure their knowledge and skills are refreshed and developed. The important message here is that all children have a *right* to a workforce that understands their obligation in ensuring the welfare and safety of the infants and young children in their care. The policy may change, but the need for a trained, knowledgeable, skilled and committed workforce that understands its collective and individual responsibility for the protection of children does not. In England, the timeframes for training were originally included in *Working Together to Safeguard Children* published in 2010 (DCSF 2010), but exact time constraints were omitted in the subsequent slimmed-down guidance. However, *Keeping Children Safe in Education* (DfE 2016b) indicated that designated persons need training every two years. In addition, all staff in the setting require training in line with the requirements of the local safeguarding children board, which is usually every three years.

Setting policy will draw on national and local guidelines; for example, in England the requirements for child protection are included in Section 3 of the EYFS in England (DfE 2017a) and in the *Working Together to Safeguard Children* documentation (DfE 2015a). These include the need for a designated person for safeguarding in every setting. In childminding settings, the childminder assumes this role. The Early Years Teacher (0–5) in England also has a specific standard to meet in relation to safeguarding. In fact, they are the only professional in England that has this focus for 0–5 explicitly built into their standards (DfE 2013a). Given the complex nature of child maltreatment, they should arguably have a lead role in settings.

Guidance has been provided in relation to the role of the designated person, also known as a lead professional, and includes liaison with the local statutory services and the local safeguarding children board, providing support and advice to staff in the setting and attending child protection training every two years. The inspections services in each of the four nations also provide a framework for settings to use. In England, Ofsted provides guidance that is updated regularly, and there are four key areas that are integral to their inspections (Ofsted 2016):

- How a culture of safeguarding is established in the setting
- Recruitment and vetting procedures
- The quality of safeguarding practice
- Arrangements for handling serious incidents and allegations.

As part of the quality of the safeguarding practice in the setting, policies also need to ensure they address issues such as how mobile phones and cameras are used in the setting. There also need to be policies about the use of social media and safe use of the internet. More recently, the *Prevent Strategy* (HM Government 2015) has placed further duties on settings in England, Wales and Scotland to work alongside young children in Early Years, '...ensuring children learn right from wrong, mix and share with other children and value other's views, know about similarities and differences between themselves and others, and challenge negative attitudes and stereotypes' (HM Government 2015, p.10).

Safeguarding and the workforce

All ECEC settings must have vetting and recruitment processes to ensure that the staff appointed, students and those working as volunteers have all undergone the appropriate processes. The DBS operates in all four nations, and there are three types of checks – basic, standard and enhanced, with a further check for those working with children part on the barred list (DBS 2017). This list includes those who have a conviction for sexual offences against children.

Settings also need to ensure that there is a policy for parents to make complaints and report concerns about staff or practice. This is often referred to as a 'whistleblowing' policy (Carr and Goosey 2017). It is a difficult and challenging area, but ultimately the safety of children cannot be compromised. The NSPCC provides a helpline for people to discuss issues confidentially, and local authorities have a designated person (DfE 2015a) to coordinate and manage this difficult area of work. In addition, concerns can be reported to the relevant inspection services. In England, for example, Ofsted would be informed either directly or through the designated person and a referral would trigger an inspection. The police may also need to be involved.

Reflection point

The importance of policy and procedures in ECEC settings cannot be emphasised enough; they should be documents that shape and develop the culture and practice in the setting. You have a personal responsibility to know about all the policies and procedures in a setting and where to find them. For those that are specifically relevant to safeguarding, all the national guidance is that, whatever your role, safeguarding is a collective and individual responsibility.

Reflect on your learning about the importance of safeguarding policies in ECEC, especially on the personal duty you have to ensure your learning and practice is constantly refreshed.

> **Exercise: Safeguarding responsibilities and roles**
> - Make a list of your responsibilities, how you will address these and what or who can help you.
> - How is the culture of safeguarding established in your workplace or placement?
> - What is your role in advocating for infants and young children to promote their wellbeing and protection?

Regardless of which country of the UK you work in, or what your role is in ECEC, you need to be familiar with the safeguarding and child protection policy and procedures of the setting in which you are working or on placement. Whatever your level of responsibility in the setting, you must refresh your knowledge and understanding regularly through training, professional discussions and keeping abreast of information in professional magazines, from the local authority and safeguarding board. For those with lead responsibilities, training and keeping up to date with research, and applying this to practice, are key continuing professional development activities.

Chapter summary

Whichever nation of the UK you reside, work or study in, the legislative and procedural frameworks for safeguarding and child protection are complicated and fluid. This chapter has introduced you to the complexities, and provided the underlying principles, references and suggestions to ensure you access the most up-to-date information to support your learning and practice.

The message in legislation and guidance is clear – that we *all* have a responsibility to protect children from harm. We need to work with other agencies, and professionals and practitioners need to ensure this happens and that information is shared in a timely and appropriate manner. ECEC offers an immense opportunity to make a real difference through ensuring that safeguarding procedures are enacted proactively and a culture of safeguarding is established. This ultimately influences relationships with other professionals, agencies, families and, most importantly, the infants and young children with whom we work.

Key learning

- The safeguarding of children is everyone's responsibility, but those working with children and young people have a duty to ensure they work with other agencies and professionals to share information if children are believed to be suffering harm or are likely to be harmed.
- The four nations of the UK have different legislative and statutory guidance, although the principles underpinning them are similar. It is important that the most recent information is accessed to ensure the most up-to-date guidance is being followed.
- Following a child protection referral, the lead responsibility usually rests with the local authority social work services. However, responding to a referral requires an inter-agency and multi-professional response.
- If the investigation leads to a Child Protection Conference, all those attending must contribute to the discussion, analysis of the information and decision-making process.
- Understanding what information can and cannot be shared is really important. The safeguarding and wellbeing of the child is paramount, and sharing factual information in a timely manner, using the right procedures, is essential.
- Most children who are abused, likely to be abused or are living in adverse conditions usually remain in the family with their parents. Intervening early is therefore important in identifying signs of abuse and providing appropriate intervention and services to families.

- There are four recognised intervention levels – universal, early help, targeted and specialist – and three main types of assessment – early help, child 'in need' and a child protection assessment, using the relevant framework.
- Assessments need to be of high quality and based on factual and detailed information to support appropriate decision-making and planning.
- Throughout the child protection process, the needs of the child are paramount, and wherever possible, supporting a child within the family should be the first priority, and legal orders only made when there is no alternative.
- Any child where an order is made should have a clear care plan in place.
- ECEC settings must have clear policies and procedures for child protection, wider safeguarding responsibilities, safe recruitment and whistleblowing.

Useful resources

For advice and guidance

The most important way to keep up to date is to use the internet to search for your local authority and their child protection procedures and the local safeguarding children board.

Legal definitions for significant harm can be found at:

- Section 31 of the *Children Act 1989* (England and Wales), www.legislation.gov.uk/ukpga/1989/41/section/31
- Articles 2 and 50 of *The Children (Northern Ireland) Order 1995*, www.legislation.gov.uk/nisi/1995/755/contents/made
- Part 2 of the *Children (Scotland) Act 1995*, www.legislation.gov.uk/ukpga/1995/36/part/II

For other useful sources of up-to-date information and useful links, see:

England, *Working Together to Safeguard Children*, www. workingtogetheronline.co.uk/index.html

England, Ofsted inspection services, www.gov.uk/government/ organisations/ofsted

Welsh Government, safeguarding legislation, policy and procedures, http://gov.wales/topics/health/socialcare/ safeguarding/?lang=en

Children in Wales, information for children, young people and families in Wales, www.childreninwales.org.uk

Scotland, Getting it Right for Every Child (GIRFEC), national policy agenda for children and young people, www.gov.scot/ Topics/People/Young-People/gettingitright

Scotland, Care Inspectorate Hub with links to relevant legislation, policy and frameworks, http://hub.careinspectorate. com/knowledge/policy-and-legislation/policy-portals/ early-years

Education Scotland, early learning and child care inspections, www.education.gov.scot/what-we-do/inspection-and-review/ about-inspections-and-reviews/Early%20learning%20and%20 childcare%20inspections

Northern Ireland, Department of Health, government web page with links to legislation policy and procedures for child protection, www.health-ni.gov.uk/topics/social-services/child-protection

NSPCC, child protection procedures and legislation for the four nations, www.nspcc.org.uk/preventing-abuse/child-protection-system

Further reading

Carr, H. and Goosey, D. (2017) *Law for Social Workers* (14th edn). Oxford: Oxford University Press. This has very clear information about all relevant legislation in England and Wales.

Chapter 7
Working with Others

Chapter objectives

By the end of this chapter you will be able to:

- Discuss the role of multi-professional working in child protection
- Know the range of professionals and practitioners involved and their role
- Explain the contribution ECEC can make to a multi-professional approach to child protection
- Understand the importance of developing skills in working in multi-professional contexts.

Introduction

Working in partnership is a central thread that runs through all aspects of child protection work and is enshrined in legislation. However, as highlighted elsewhere in this book, SCRs frequently illustrate how a lack of communication and information sharing can 'contribute to the deaths or serious injuries of children'

(DfE 2015a, p.16). In other words, regardless of legal requirements, statutory guidance and local procedures and protocols, collaborative working can be very difficult, with potentially fatal consequences. Furthermore, recent research has suggested that the complexities of collaborative working can lead to children being invisible in the child protection process (Ferguson 2017).

Professionals and practitioners working or planning to work in ECEC must understand their responsibilities for all aspects of safeguarding and protecting children. These include developing skills in working with others, both in the setting and with external agencies. They also need to advocate for the infants and young children in their care. As highlighted previously in this book, unlike other professionals, those working in ECEC spend considerable time with infants and young children over a sustained period. Consequently, they have different insights to bring to investigations and assessments.

This chapter builds on Chapter 6, focusing specifically on the statutory requirement for collaborative working and sharing information. The language used to describe working together is discussed as well as the strengths and challenges of partnership working. The knowledge and skills required in multi-professional working to promote the safeguarding of all children is also considered.

Language of working together

The opening paragraph of this chapter used a range of terms to refer to inter-agency and multi-professional working, indicating that this area of work has no single definition. Terms are used interchangeably and can mean different things in different sectors of the children's workforce (Lumsden 2014). In child protection, 'inter-agency' is the term usually used to describe the different agencies that need to work together, for example, health, social care, education, Early Years, housing and the police. In England, the agencies and individuals involved in child protection are contained in Section 11 of the *Children Act 2004* (DfE 2015a).

Each individual brings his or her specific discipline, knowledge and skills to the multi-professional approach to child protection. For example, social workers, health visitors, midwives, family workers, police officers, head teachers or Early Years Teachers (0–5) may work together to share knowledge and develop an action plan for intervention. The impact of so many practitioners and professionals involved in a family is addressed later in the chapter.

For the purposes of this chapter, 'collaboration' is used as an umbrella term for practitioners and professionals from different, or the same, agency, working together. The Child Protection Conference is an example of when all those involved with the child and family who are being investigated collaborate together to analyse, discuss and make decisions about what action needs to be taken. This collaboration can also be termed 'integrated working'. The child should always be the central focus of discussions (Lumsden 2014). Those providing the core intervention with the family are known as the *Team Around the Family* (TAF) or the *Team Around the Child* (TAC).

Team Around the Child/Family

This section considers the roles of some of the main professional groups that work together to protect children. The number of individuals working with a family can be considerable, leading to confusion, duplication and miscommunication between agencies and the professionals and practitioners working in them. Therefore, a key practice skill is the ability to communicate clearly and effectively with others, whatever their age or status. However, communication is also influenced by the structures and cultures in different organisations and power imbalances that occur within them (Lumsden 2014). Sometimes the actual needs, feelings and impact on the family involved can get missed. Furthermore, their responses and behaviours can be misinterpreted. The following case study and exercise provide an opportunity for you to reflect on this from your own perspective and that of the mother.

CASE STUDY: KELLIE AND CILLA

Gemma, the mother, aged 22, and Tony, the father, aged 21, have known each other since school and have lived together since the birth of their first child, Kellie, aged four. They have another daughter, Cilla, aged 18 months, and Gemma is pregnant with their third child. Gemma's mother, father and elder sister live close by, and regularly take the children to and from nursery. Kellie often spends weekends with her grandparents.

The family live in an area of disadvantage, with low rates of social mobility and high rates of unemployment and families living in poverty. Neither Tony nor Gemma is working and they have financial and relationship difficulties. There has been ongoing police involvement for repeated reporting of domestic violence.

Tony is currently on probation having served a six-month sentence for theft. This was his second period in prison. He has also has received a number of previous cautions as well as being banned from driving for being under the influence of alcohol. The police are currently investigating him in relation to a number of local burglaries.

Kellie and Cilla attend the local nursery. They both have separate key workers and Kellie is receiving speech therapy for language delay. There are also concerns about Cilla's development as she is underweight and small for her age. The health visitor, in consultation with their family doctor, has referred Cilla to the local paediatric services. She is currently undergoing a number of tests. Cilla has, however, missed her last two appointments.

Gemma is having a difficult pregnancy, and there are concerns she will not go to full term. Her midwife is worried that she needs additional assistance and may have prenatal depression. She has referred her, via the family doctor, for an assessment to the local psychiatric services.

A family worker based at the local children's centre works with the family and Home Start, a local charity, has a volunteer who visits at tea time three times a week. The family worker is concerned about child protection and has just made a referral to the local MASH. She is worried that the children are being neglected and experiencing emotional abuse because of the arguments they are witnessing. The Home Start volunteer has also reported her concerns about Gemma's difficulties in managing the children's behaviour, and her difficulties in responding positively to them when they seek her attention. Tony is never at home on the days she visits.

Exercise: Team Around the Family

- Make a list of those involved with the family under the following headings: 'Agencies and services', 'Professionals, practitioners and volunteers', and 'Parents and extended family members':
  - What do you think may be the barriers to information sharing in this case?
  - How would you feel if you were Gemma?
- What would it be like if you had to share information about yourself, your background and family with professionals?
- Would you fully understand the role of everyone you had to work with?
- How would your pregnancy and wider physical and mental health issues impact on your ability to relate to all of those involved in your life – your children, as well as those working with you?
- How do you think having a full assessment would be helpful to the family?

Table 7.1 provides an overview of the agencies and services and professionals, practitioners and volunteers involved with the family. It is easy to see how overwhelming having so many agencies and people to interact with could be for the family, and how difficult it could be for the lead agency to obtain all the relevant information for a child protection assessment. These challenges reinforce the importance of a coordinated approach that promotes the wellbeing of children and parents experiencing difficulties (Taylor and Thoburn 2016). Families with such complex needs require a '...high quality single-disciplinary services but also well-coordinated services from a range of professionals. A "team around the family approach" is now recognised as an essential working model for the effective provision of educative, therapeutic and placement services' (Taylor and Thoburn 2016, p.1).

Table 7.1: Agencies and services and professionals, practitioners and volunteers involved with the family

Agencies and services	Professionals, practitioners and volunteers	Family
Health	Midwife	Mother
Education	Paediatrician	Father
Social care	Health visitor	Aunt
ECEC settings	Doctor	Grandmother
Probation	Psychiatrist	Grandfather
Police	Speech therapist	
MASH team	Social worker	
Children centre	Probation officer	
Home Start	Police officers	
(charity)	Two ECEC practitioners (Key Person)	
	Designated person	
	Family worker	
	Home Start worker	
	Home Start volunteer	

Reflection point

How did your list compare to the list above?

Do you know the role of each of these professionals and practitioners?

Exercise: Using theory in working with families

Using the bio-ecological theory presented earlier, in Chapter 1, revisit the Kellie and Cilla case study earlier in the chapter, and undertake the following tasks:

- Draw the concentric circle framework.
- In each of the systems write the people, agencies and policy and procedures that are involved with the family or that influence family life.
- In the *macrosystem* write the policy and legislation that is influencing the work of agencies working with the family.
- Reflect on how the *chronosystem* and *chaotic-system* provide greater insights and understanding of the children's development.

Your diagram should help you visualise those working with the family in a different way, illustrating the raft of professionals, practitioners and family (*mesosystem*) who are located within the *microsystem*. All the agencies and their respective policies and procedures will be in the *exosystem*, and at a macro level is the legislation, statutory guidance and policy discussed in Chapter 6. You will be able to see how over time (*chronosystem*) further insights have been gained into the relationship between Gemma and Tony, and how this is affecting the development of their children.

Furthermore, the *chaotic-system* enables greater understanding of how events in the family and outside may impact on the family, including events internal to the family such as depression, drug taking and criminal behaviour and imprisonment. Externally the family can be affected by changes at a policy level that impact on services that are available at a local level. In the *microsystem*, there may be changes in the professionals and practitioners working with Gemma and her family.

Another factor that can influence what is happening in the *microsystem* are the challenges in collaborative working in child protection cases. In the case study, you have learnt about the number of professionals, practitioners and agencies that can be involved with one family. This can be overwhelming and lead to miscommunication, duplication of services and a lack of information sharing. Furthermore, those working with the family do not always fully understand each others' training, roles and responsibilities or where their services overlap. For example, a family worker, social worker and health visitor may have all been intervening separately with a family but have all focused on the same areas, such as parenting skills and nutrition. This is confusing for the family, especially if they all give different advice, and it is also a waste of resources. Consequently, one of the benefits from a TAF approach should be that it mitigates against duplication of services. There should also be a reduction in the number of people that the family has to interact with. Furthermore, the family should know exactly who is working with them and their respective remits.

Professionals and practitioners involved in child protection

This section provides a brief outline of some of the main professionals and practitioners working together in child protection cases.

Social worker: Requires an undergraduate or postgraduate degree in social work and has to be registered to practice. They have professional requirements to meet in order to maintain their registration and have a code of ethics to follow. They can work in a range of specialist areas such as child protection, fostering, adoption, mental health, learning disability and elder care. Social workers are employed in a range of agencies including local authorities, voluntary agencies and charities (British Association of Social Workers (BASW) 2017). In child protection cases, the local authority social worker is the lead professional. They have responsibility for the child protection assessment and leading on subsequent assistance for the family, court proceedings and the care plan for the child. The social worker who made the initial assessment is unlikely to continue if longer-term involvement is required. Each local authority will have its own structure and terminology.

Midwife: Assists a mother throughout pregnancy and up to about 14 days after birth, depending on the particular circumstances of each case. They are located in hospitals on the labour ward or attached to a health centre in the community. They have to be registered with the Nursing and Midwifery Council (NMC) and have studied at graduate level (Royal College of Midwives 2017). In relation to child protection, the midwife responsible for the mother's care during pregnancy will have valuable information to share about health and other issues, such as family relationships and the home environment. This is especially important in cases where there is a pre-birth conference to consider whether the baby should be subject to a Court Order following birth.

Health visitor: A trained nurse or midwife who has undertaken postgraduate training. They have an important role working with parents to ensure the best start for the child and to offer advice on all aspects of child development and parenting. They refer to relevant agencies as appropriate. They take over the care for the newborn baby from the midwife and should work with the family until a child is aged five. At this point the school nurse becomes involved. The health visitor can often be the first to recognise child protection issues and they are an important part of any child protection investigation. They will normally have crucial information to contribute to the assessment process, and are a vital member of the TAF (NHS 2017c).

School nurse: A qualified nurse or midwife who undertakes additional training in public health. They take over responsibility for the child when they start school and undertake a health assessment in reception year. They are usually linked to several schools to promote the health and wellbeing of children and young people (aged 5–19) (Direct Gov.uk 2017). Alongside their other health colleagues, they have an important role in child protection, from early detection to being a member of the core team assessing and assisting the family. They may have particular health information that enables a fuller understanding of the health and wellbeing needs of a child.

General practitioner (GP): The role of the GP is one we are all familiar with. They work in the community in practices usually located in health centres with other members of the primary health care team. Their training includes a focus on child protection, and they are in a prime position to identify signs of abuse and will have a picture of specific issues that develop over a period of time. They also work closely with health visitors and midwives.

Police surgeon: They are usually GPs who also work with the police. They can have a specific role in undertaking medicals on children who are suspected of being abused.

Police: The police have primary responsibility for the detection and prosecution of perpetrators of crime. There are various entry routes and roles in the service. In child protection cases their main role is to investigate whether a crime has been committed and to gather evidence for prosecution. There are specific teams that deal with child abuse, family violence and wider safeguarding issues. More recently they have become part of MASH teams. There are also part of teams that focus on sexual exploitation and internet abuse locally, nationally and internationally. At a Child Protection Conference they can ask for a private session to discuss issues that may jeopardise an inquiry if the family know about them (College of Policing 2017).

Early Years Teacher (0–5): In England the Early Years Teacher (0–5) (formerly known as an Early Years Professional) is a graduate who has undertaken specific professional training to be awarded the status Early Years Teacher Status (EYTS) (DfE 2017b). They should be ideally placed to lead on child protection and working with others, as these are part of the professional standards they have to meet. However, their role in settings is still emerging, and the lead person in an ECEC setting may be someone else. In child protection their knowledge, understanding and practice skills in child development, their understanding of diversity, disadvantage, child maltreatment and how children learn make them ideally placed to contribute to the investigation and assessment of the family and child. They should also be able to reflect on the particular child's needs and ensure the ECEC environment and learning opportunities are appropriate.

Designated safeguarding person in ECEC settings: The provision of ECEC in the UK is a mixture of home care (childminders), group care (usually provided by the private, voluntary or independent sector) and State-maintained nurseries, as well as children's centres. There is a vast range of roles, titles and qualifications in these settings, and in group care those working directly with the children are usually qualified at Level 2 or 3. All staff must have training in safeguarding, but there is a specific role that has the lead for safeguarding. This member of staff is usually qualified from Level 3 upwards and, in England, the Early Years Teacher (0–5) has real strengths to bring to this role.

The role of the designated person for safeguarding includes (DfE 2016b):

- Ensuring staff know how to raise concerns and the signs and symptoms of child abuse and neglect.
- Knowing how to refer any concerns to the relevant people and services.
- Monitoring children who are the subject of Child Protection Plans.
- Maintaining accurate and secure child protection records.

Head teacher/teacher in schools: Usually holds a professional teaching qualification at undergraduate or postgraduate level. All education establishments have to have a designated person for safeguarding who is a senior member of staff, and in maintained nurseries and primary schools this is often the head teacher. Their roles are the same as the lead person in ECEC, and they are required to have training every two years. They must be fully aware of all the local policies and procedures (DfE 2016b).

Teaching assistant: Does not need formal qualifications, although many will have a teaching assistant qualification or higher. They work in the classroom alongside the teacher and often have responsibility for specific children who may have additional needs. They have an important role in the initial detection of abuse and ongoing assistance for children in the classroom who are involved in an assessment or who are already in local authority care.

Family worker: Located in a range of settings, including children's centres, social work teams, nurseries, probation and increasingly in schools. They require some form of qualification in education, health or social care, but are not registered professionals.

Family workers engage directly with the family, providing a range of interventions including practical assistance, advice and guidance. They may focus on parenting skills and enabling families to understand and respond appropriately to the developmental needs of their child. Family workers may also provide advice and guidance on home management and have an important role in all aspects of detection, assessment and subsequent intervention in child protection cases. They should be a member of the TAF and TAC (National Careers Service 2017b).

Children's guardian: A qualified social worker employed by the Children and Family Court Advisory and Support Service (Cafcass). They are independent of the local authority and are appointed in cases where a Court Order is being sought to ensure the safety of the child, and when their best interests are served through a Court Order. They also have to ensure the child's rights are represented and will appoint a solicitor on the child's behalf. They complete a report for court about the best interests for the child based on an assessment undertaken through interviews with the family and professionals involved (Cafcass 2017).

In addition to the professionals and practitioners listed in Table 7.1, other individuals can be involved from, for example, the housing department, Child and Adolescent Mental Health Services (CAMHS) and probation services.

Reflection point

What do you think are the challenges of having so many different professionals involved in child protection cases?

A knowledge base for multi-professionals working in child protection

Traditionally, professions in the UK have developed as entities in their own right, with a specific knowledge base and professional identity (see Figure 7.1). Many have precise entry requirements and continuing professional development requirements, as discussed in Chapter 1. However, the unique needs of children and their families cannot easily be separated into distinct areas and, as discussed previously, a holistic approach is required where agencies, professionals and practitioners work together.

In child protection, professionals and practitioners work together in a range of ways, bringing their knowledge in a specific discipline either to contribute to the team working with the family and child or as actual members of a multi-professional team. Figure 7.1 shows what single professional working and integrated working looks like. The central area of overlap in the *zone of integrated working* has permeable borders and is a flexible space that promotes inclusivity and integration, a space where professionals and practitioners come together and share and develop new knowledge and skills, as well as developing a greater shared understanding of working in complex situations. In child protection assessments those who work in this zone can identify the strengths of the family as well as the challenges they are facing.

While working in this flexible space has immense benefits, there are also challenges for the individual. These include issues around professional identity and role confusion that occur when others in the team undertake some of the traditional roles of their professional remit (Anning *et al.* 2010). If new models of working are not embraced and power imbalances between different professionals addressed, barriers to integrated working develop.

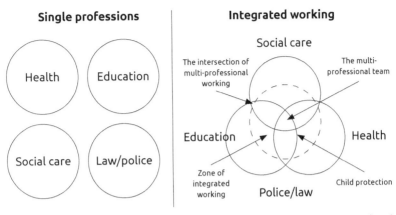

Source: Based on Lumsden (2012)

Figure 7.1: Single professions and integrated working

Exercise: Zone of integrated working
- Make a list of what you think the knowledge and skills are for working in the zone of integrated working.

In order to work in this *zone*, professionals need:

- A sound knowledge and understanding of their own specific area of expertise
- To recognise the importance of integrated working
- To know how to work in inter-disciplinary and multi-professional teams
- An understanding of what it means to be inter-professional.

In health and social care, inter-professional training is embedded into professional training, and involves how to learn and work together. Those working in ECEC also need a breadth of skills in this area as they work in a range of teams, with parents and alongside verbal and non-verbal children. They also have to engage with other agencies and professionals. In England, working with others is integrated into the Early Years Teacher (0–5) training, and they have a specific standard to meet in this area.

Table 7.2: Core knowledge and skills for integrated working

Knowledge	Skills
What is a team?	Team worker
Effective team working	Communication skills:
Being a member of a team	• Active listening
Leadership styles	• Presenting
Different types of teams	• Writing
Subject knowledge	• Telephone
Knowledge of other professional roles	• Sending professional emails
Anti-discriminatory practice	Makes positive, professional relationships
Reflective practice models	Openness to learn from others
Policy, procedures and protocols	Emotional intelligence
Understanding how different agencies work	Empathetic
Research findings	Diplomatic
	Supportive
	Confident
	Assertive
	Organised
	Reflective

The lists in Table 7.2 are not conclusive, although they do provide a clear indication of the depth of knowledge and range of skills required for integrated working. It is through the continual development of knowledge and skills that professionals can move from novice to expert in working multi-professionally in the complex area of child protection.

Practice point: From novice to expert

In the UK, Early Childhood programmes are mapped on to the *Subject Benchmark Statement: Early Childhood Studies* (QAA 2014). This clearly lays out the knowledge, understanding and skills that underpin the holistic study of young children aged 0–8.

The study of Early Childhood is inter-disciplinary and includes all aspects of child development, health and wellbeing, safeguarding and child abuse, in particular, early learning, policy, diversity and disadvantage, reflective practice and working with others. In addition, there is a focus on professional and personal development, working in teams and developing competence in all aspects of observing children and planning.

It is important to remember that new graduates and professionals are not experts. They require guidance, mentoring and further training to develop their skills from novice to expert. Most importantly, in any work with children and families, especially child protection, there is always something new to learn and different viewpoints to be considered. It is also important to keep abreast of research findings and SCR inquiries as these help to shape and extend our practice.

Exercise: Skills in integrated working

- Compile a list of how you believe knowledge, understanding and skills you are developing will assist you in contributing to the child protection assessment and work of the core team.
- Using the core knowledge and skills for integrated working, reflect on your current knowledge and skills. How do you think this will enable you to contribute to an integrated approach to child protection?

Role of ECEC in working with others in child protection

While ECEC is an occupation and profession that continues to have low status (Marsden, McMahon and Younde 2014), there is an increasing focus on qualifications and the knowledge required by practitioners from Level 2 onwards. There has also been an increased focus across the UK on graduate and professional programmes in ECEC. The move to graduate leaders means that there are staff with professional training in child abuse and working with others who have much to offer in the field of child protection. Furthermore, they are competent in observations and assessing the social emotional development and learning of infants and young children (Lumsden 2012; Marsden *et al.* 2014). In other words, there are skilled and knowledgeable practitioners and professionals working in ECEC who can effectively contribute to the child protection assessment and subsequent intervention. However, not all the different professions working in the zone of integrated working are aware of these changes.

The ECEC profession needs to become more confident in articulating what it can contribute to child protection processes. Training needs to ensure that students are provided with opportunities to develop their confidence and communication skills. They also need to learn about theory and how to apply this in practice. An exemplar here is the child protection role-play assignment that students studying at the University of Northampton undertake (Taylor, Whiting and Sharland 2008).

Exercise: Child Protection Conference role-play

This role-play exercise is a useful example of how students' understanding about the strengths and challenges in multi-professional can be developed. The students participate in a simulated conference with a formal chair, which involves the following:

- The students are allocated a specific professional or practitioner role, information about their role and whom they need to communicate and share information with.
- They research their role and preferably meet with a professional or practitioner who is employed in the role.
- They use the information they have been given and gained from their collaboration with others, to participate in information sharing and decision-making at the conference.
- The week after the role-play the students participate in a collaborative learning exercise to reflect on their learning and what it means for their future practice.

The role-play enables students to develop:

- Confidence in their own presentation skills in an inter-disciplinary and multi-professional forum that involves a range of agencies
- Knowledge and understanding of professional roles in child protection
- An appreciation of the challenges in sharing information, including the difficulty of arranging meetings to actually share information
- The challenges of assimilating a large amount of information and then making a decision in a short space of time
- Understanding of the power imbalances that are inherent in child protection and the experience of the birth family.

Year on year, feedback from students indicates that this is the most challenging and enjoyable assignment they complete. Former students often recall this as one of the experiences they remember, and indicate how it has influenced their professional practice. Their learning about the importance of how much and what information is shared, how it is shared, power imbalances and the position of the parents and child at the conference is profound. They experience at first hand the process of 'putting the jigsaw' together, enabling them to recognise the value of information sharing, the challenges and importance of processing complex information in a short time, and that no one professional has all the information about a child, their family and the environment in which they live.

Reflection point
How do you think you can prepare yourself for working collaboratively with others and developing the confidence, knowledge and skills to represent the children and families you work with in the area of child protection?

Chapter summary

This chapter has given a brief introduction to working with others to safeguard children. It contends that those working in ECEC have a vital role in the multi-professional team that enhances the assessment and subsequent core work with the child and family. They are in the unique position of being directly responsible for the care and early learning of those using their particular setting, as well as working in partnership with their families. Therefore, students and trainees for EYTS in England need to develop their skills and confidence in working in a range of teams, with other agencies and parents and carers. They need to know about their role in safeguarding all children and sharing information in child protection cases. Finally, it is important that the strengths and challenges of multi-professional working are understood, and that this knowledge is used to influence practice and to improve outcomes for children and their families.

Key learning

- There is no one definition for working with others, with terms often used interchangeably.
- Multi-professional work takes place in the zone of integrated working and requires specific knowledge and skills in working in a range of teams and with different practitioners and professionals, as well as with the family.
- Collaborative working strengthens the child protection information-sharing and assessment processes. However, it can be challenging, and there are substantial barriers to effective communication between agencies and professionals. The introduction of MASH teams, where representatives for a range of agencies are co-located together, is one way that these issues can be addressed.
- ECEC is an important partner in all child protection processes. They have knowledge, understanding and skills in the holistic development of infants and young children, including a range of communication and observation skills.
- It is important that those studying and in professional training in Early Childhood have opportunities not only to gain the knowledge they need, but also to build their confidence levels for presenting themselves in professional contexts.

Useful resources

For advice and guidance
There are several short films on YouTube that discuss and illustrate Child Protection Conference scenarios including Bournemouth University (2017) and LCSB (2017).

Further reading

Lumsden, E. (2014) 'Joined-Up Thinking in Practice: An Exploration of Professional Collaboration.' In T. Waller and G. Davis (eds) *An Introduction to Early Childhood: A Multidisciplinary Approach* (3rd edn). London: Sage. This chapter explores the benefits and challenges of multi-professional working.

Davies, J. and Smith, M. (2012) *Working in Multi-professional Contexts.* London: Sage. This book considers the knowledge and skills required to work in a multi-professional context. There are useful exercises to develop your practice skills in this important area of professional practice.

Chapter 8

Creating the Right Environment

Chapter objectives

By the end of this chapter you will be able to:
- Explain how to create nurturing environments that are sensitive to and promote the holistic development of children experiencing early trauma
- Apply frameworks to promote a whole-setting approach that facilitates pedagogical conversations
- Recognise and act on personal responsibility for continuing professional development.

Introduction

There is clear evidence that high-quality Early Childhood provision positively promotes the holistic development of infants and young children, laying the foundations on which to build. However, there is no legal obligation to attend ECEC, and some children and families living in adverse situations do not access services. Consequently, those working in ECEC settings cannot directly change the environments in which children live, but they *do* have responsibility for their own professional practice and for that of the setting. As Percival (2014) rightly argued, how we bring the duties of safeguarding alive in ECEC is our choice. If outcomes for children are to improve, the wider safeguarding and welfare duties placed on ECEC through legislation must become more than an audit of compliance. To achieve this, the important role of graduate leadership in ECEC cannot be underestimated, and nor can the significance of the culture and ethos of the setting.

The overarching aim of this chapter is therefore to challenge you to think differently about practice. There is consideration of how the needs of children experiencing abuse or living in adverse environments are addressed through pedagogy and a curriculum framework. There is also a specific focus on safe practice, focusing on your own responsibility for personal and professional development. Case examples are used to spark ideas for reflective and attuned practice. You will also be encouraged to apply research, theory and practice wisdom to your work through the use of the *Unique Childhoods Model* (see Figure 8.1).

Introducing the Unique Childhoods Model

The Unique Childhoods Model is about driving change at a community level for infants, young children and families to improve their future outcomes and opportunities. It is presented as a flexible framework to analyse, critique and reflect on practice. It aims to prompt new ways of thinking and working to strengthen engagement with infants, young children and their families. The model comprises eight *threads of practice* (see Figure 8.1) and eight *threads of change* (see Figure 8.2), reflecting the interconnectedness of the different areas of ECEC practice and specific strands, such as child protection, that need addressing.

The holistic needs of the child are always at the centre, and the model can be used to:

- Facilitate a 'helicopter' view of what is happening in the whole setting (see Table 8.1)

- Focus on a specific area of practice (see the exercise in the next section and Christopher's case study).

The model encourages pedagogical conversations with children, parents, caregivers and other professionals, and provides a framework to reflect on your own learning and development. For the purpose of this chapter, it is mainly used as a framework:

- To focus on child protection
- To explore how the needs of specific children are addressed
- As a tool to reflect on professional development.

Figure 8.1: Unique Childhoods Model: Threads of practice

Figure 8.2: Unique Childhoods Model: Threads of change

The Unique Childhoods Model evolved from working alongside students and research into the development of a new professional identity in ECEC and the professional capabilities of the then called Early Years Professional (now the Early Years Teacher) (Lumsden 2012). Rapid development in the inter-disciplinary subject area of Early Childhood, alongside new professional standards, means that students and trainees need guidance to enable them to 'make sense' of the academic field and how it relates to the mixed economy of ECEC. This includes understanding how different settings operate, as well as a deeper appreciation of the unique needs of children and how to apply theory and research to practice.

ECEC has also become more complicated to lead and manage, both administratively and pedagogically, and actually ensuring the child remains central is not always easy. While inspection regimes are important, they have added another layer to this. As discussed elsewhere in this book, the child can become invisible in the child protection process, and it is vital that this does not happen in ECEC – the Unique Childhoods Model introduced in this chapter offers a framework to ensure this is not the case.

Table 8.1: Overview of setting practice

Threads of practice	Overarching focus
Values	Values underpinning the ethos and practice of the setting.
Pedagogy	The pedagogic approach to teaching, educating and caregiving. This includes social and emotional development as well as cognition.
Leadership	High-level leadership and management as well as how the specific areas of the setting are managed and led.

Threads of practice	Overarching focus
Staff	Characteristics of the adults working in the setting, including volunteers. For example, what are the training qualifications, gender, ages, specific roles and continuing professional development opportunities?
Progress	How is the progress of the setting, children and staff monitored and evaluated? How are specific intervention strategies evaluated and learning used to enhance practice?
Research	How are research findings applied to practice and disseminated to staff?
Budget	How is the budget used? For example, how much is spent on staff development and addressing focused work with infants and young children living in adverse circumstances?
Compliance	How is the child central to all the different compliance requirements and inspection frameworks the setting has to meet?

Pedagogy and child protection

Debates about pedagogy in ECEC are far-reaching, and at the end of this chapter you will find a 'Further reading' section to extend your knowledge of this area. Broadly, pedagogy in ECEC is concerned with how the adult utilises the science and art of teaching, educating and caregiving to facilitate planning, learning, skill development and attitudes that are respectful and sensitive (Siraj-Blatchford *et al.* 2002; Wall, Litjens and Taguma 2015). A pedagogical or educational approach 'explains the roles of the staff, the materials and space, the appropriate pedagogy (practices), and in some cases, the learning objectives'

(Wall *et al.* 2015, p.40). The total opposite of this was found in the *Little Ted's Inquiry,* which stated:

> These findings clearly evidence that child protection policy was not seen as an integral part of the settings pedagogy. Rather there was a compliance approach which was not integrated into the settings practice. There was also no recognition that the intimate care needs of infants and young children are integral to pedagogy and staff training. If settings are to be attuned to the needs of children facing adverse life experiences the pedagogical approach should apply theory and research to practice, compliance will then follow. (Plymouth Safeguarding Children Board 2010, p.20)

The philosophy underpinning the pedagogy also needs to be evident in all aspects of the setting's approach. It needs to be flexible, enabling planning to start with how the child presents each day. In other words, planning needs to be 'in the moment', and professionals and practitioners need to understand that the behaviour of a child experiencing trauma can be erratic, for no apparent reason.

There also need to be abundant opportunities to promote learning through play that encourages self-awareness, awareness of others and self-management. All children, but especially those experiencing adversity, need to be enabled to develop their interpersonal and practical skills, recognise their abilities and, most importantly, the consequences of their actions. They also need to learn how to problem-solve, recognise feelings and how to regulate their own behaviour, as well as developing resilience and having opportunities that promote their physical growth, health and language development. For the majority of children, their parents and caregivers play a vital role in these areas. For those infants and young children who experience abuse and inconsistency at home, especially when their holistic development has been impeded, laying these vital foundations is far more challenging.

Reflection point

With a specific focus on infants and young children who are experiencing adverse home environments or who are subject to Child Protection Plans, how does your workplace or placement:

- Organise planning?
- Address social and emotional development?
- Provide opportunities that foster the development of resilience?
- Promote physical development and health?

How easy has it been to answer these questions?

What do you think your setting could do differently?

The role of professional leadership in directing setting approaches and promoting practice in these areas is imperative. In England, the Early Years Teacher (0–5) should be leading in this area. They are the only professional in England with standards to meet in safeguarding in 0–5 and working with others (DfE 2013a). Those working in ECEC also reflect a wide age range, various qualifications and experience. Consequently, there are vast variations in the skills and ability to apply knowledge to practice. This further reinforces the importance of strong pedagogical professional leadership. Regardless of where we work in the UK, we should be striving for an ECEC workforce that is secure in their pedagogical approach, confident in their knowledge and skills and who know how to articulate these professionally. Professionals and practitioners need to use their knowledge and skills to work alongside parents, enabling them to deepen their understanding and skills in meeting the ongoing development needs of their child. They also need to contribute to the assessments that support a fuller understanding of the child, their environment and developmental needs, as discussed earlier, in Chapter 5.

The following exercise introduces you to using the framework presented at the start of this chapter to analyse, critique and reflect on how your workplace or placement setting addresses the needs of children requiring protection.

Exercise: Unique Childhoods Model and child protection

Use a separate boxed section for each area. Using the Unique Childhoods Model and the questions below, reflect on how your placement or workplace addresses its responsibilities for child protection.

Values
- What are the values underpinning practice in the setting?
- How do you know what the values of the setting are?
- How do children, families and other professionals know what these are?
- How do the values reflect the settings approach to children, their health, wellbeing and safety?
- How do the values reflect how the setting works with parents or caregivers and other professionals?
- Are parents and carers welcomed into the setting?
- Is there a culture of professional development or a blame culture?

Pedagogy
- What is the philosophy underpinning the pedagogical approaches in the setting?
- How is the pedagogy of the setting used to support and nurture those experiencing the full range of adverse life experiences to learn and to develop new skills and attitudes?
- How are the characteristics of effective learning evident in practice?

- How are these used to enable those who have experienced abuse or who live in adverse environments to have the foundations for later learning?
- How is the social and emotional development, as well as early learning needs, of the child met?
- Infants and young children need to be comforted as well as have their intimate care needs, such as toileting, met. How is this area reflected in the pedagogy of the setting?
- How does the setting explain the pedagogy to parents and support their understanding of their child's ongoing developmental needs?
- How is the pedagogical approach explained to other professionals?

Leadership

- Do you know who has what leadership role in the setting?
- Do you know who to go to for advice and support?
- How do the leaders model good practice?
- How do the leaders engage with other professionals and agencies?
- How does the setting lead on child protection and the wider safeguarding agenda?
- How do those working in the setting, parents or caregivers and other professionals know who has the designated lead for child protection?

Staff

- How does the induction process address child protection?
- What initial and ongoing training is provided about child abuse?
- How do staff know what the policies and procedures are in the setting and who has responsibility for what?
- How is supervision used to develop staff?

- What ongoing training is provided to staff working with parents or caregivers and other professionals?
- Are the adults in the setting respectful to one another, the children and their families?
- Do they listen to children?
- Are they encouraged to challenge and develop practice?

Progress

- How is the progress made by the infants and young children monitored?
- What measures are specifically taken to assess, monitor and plan for children who are known to be experiencing abuse or are living in adverse environments?
- How is progress shared with parents and carers?

Research

- Does the setting undertake any research into how their pedagogical approaches with children enhance their outcomes?
- How is research into child abuse, adverse life experiences and attachment used to support the pedagogical practices in the setting?

Budget

- How is funding used to support children in need and those known to be at risk of harm or in the care of the local authority?
- How much funding does the setting use on all training?
- How much funding is allocated to child protection training?

Compliance

- How does the setting meet the statutory and regulatory requirements for child protection?

- How does it ensure that the setting is compliant for the relevant inspection regimes?
- What are the policies and protocols of the setting for reporting concerns about abuse whistleblowing and safe recruitment?
- What Prevent policies and training are in place?

Reflection point

Have you been able to answer all these questions?

How have they helped you develop a greater understanding of how the needs of the unique child are being met in the setting?

What areas do you think can be improved on and how?

Are any questions missing?

Extension activity: Threads of change

Use the Unique Childhoods Model and the questions for each area to explore how the setting addresses the areas below to develop a holistic understanding of how the unique needs of all children are met:

- Attachment
- Poverty
- Inclusion
- Health and wellbeing
- Children's mental health
- Work with families.

Curriculum frameworks and safeguarding and wellbeing in ECEC

With the expansion of ECEC provision and greater political involvement, curriculum frameworks have been introduced to support learning and development in ECEC. England, Wales, Scotland and Northern Ireland all have their own frameworks, but underpinning them is an integrated play-based approach to early learning and development, and the importance of promoting the health and safety of all children. The specific links to the different frameworks can be found at the end of this chapter.

This section draws on the EYFS in England (DfE 2017a). The principles of every child being 'unique', the importance of 'positive relationships' and 'enabling environments' as well as the fact that 'children develop and learn in different ways...at different rates' (DfE 2017a, p.5) have relevance to all areas of the UK. These four principles are reinforced by the safeguarding and welfare requirements of the EYFS, which states:

> Children learn best when they are healthy, safe and secure, when their individual needs are met, and when they have positive relationships with the adults caring for them. The safeguarding and welfare requirements...are designed to help providers create high quality settings which are welcoming, safe and stimulating, and where children are able to enjoy learning and grow in confidence. (DfE 2017a, p.15)

Furthermore, the EYFS (2017a, p.5) also aims to provide:

- Quality and consistency in all Early Years settings, so that every child makes good progress and no child gets left behind
- A secure foundation through learning and development opportunities that are planned around the needs and interests of each individual child and that are assessed and reviewed regularly

- Partnership working between practitioners and with parents and/or carers
- Equality of opportunity and anti-discriminatory practice, ensuring that every child is included and supported.

Actually making these words reality is complex. For many children, the period from conception to the age of two can have a profound effect on their future trajectory. If the child then attends a setting that is not attuned to their needs or able to apply knowledge and research to practice; redressing the attainment gap is not even an aspiration (Ofsted 2016).

It is therefore essential that the pedagogy underpinning the setting is applied in practice. The EYFS identifies the characteristics of effective learning and the prime and specific areas of learning that form part of the EYFS profile at the end of the Foundation Years (DfE 2016) (see Table 8.2). These provide an excellent framework to specifically explore the pedagogy strand of the Unique Childhoods Model introduced in the previous section.

Table 8.2: Characteristics and areas of effective learning and development

Characteristics of effective learning	Areas of learning and development	
Active learning Creating and thinking critically Playing and exploring	**Prime areas**	Personal, social and emotional development Physical development Communication and language
	Specific Areas	Literacy Mathematics Understanding the world Expressive arts and design

Key Person

To ensure that the unique needs of each child are addressed, settings should have a Key Person system, and a Key Person model has been evident in settings from the 1980s onwards (Johnson 2016). This role was formalised in the EYFS.

The Key Person has a number of children for whom they are responsible. The exact number is not specified, but there is a specific adult to child ratio in force. Given that this is a complex and emotionally demanding role, it would seem advisable that the number of children a Key Person has is in line with ratio requirements. In reality, this is not the case, however, and there is a huge variation in the number of children a Key Person is responsible for, with no tracking of this by any inspection regime.

Exercise: Key Person responsibilities

In your workplace or placement, explore the following:

- What are the roles and responsibilities of the Key Person?
- What qualification level is the Key Person?
- How many children do they have responsibility for?
- What is the age range of the children they have responsibility for?
- How is the Key Person chosen?
- Do the children have a voice in selecting them?
- What happens if the Key Person does not form a relationship with the child?
- Is there more than one Key Person?
- How are holidays or sickness managed for the child?
- How is the Key Person supervised?

Talk to other students to find out their experience in relation to these questions.

The responsibilities of the Key Person should include supporting the transition into the setting and home each day, building relationships, creating enabling environments to promote a secure base and information sharing. They are the person who should be an attachment figure for the child, someone who holds them in mind, works at seeing the world through their eyes and responds to them when they are distressed (see Chapter 3) (DfE 2017a). They also need to recognise changes in behaviour and physical appearance as well as actually responding effectively to the child's needs (Johnson 2016). In order to fulfil their responsibilities, they require appropriate knowledge and skills as well as ongoing training. They need to be aware of contemporary research, especially around brain development, attachment, child abuse and neglect, as well as the impact of living in adverse environments. The importance of continuing professional development is addressed in the section on 'Safe practice' below.

Reflection point

Drawing on your learning, practice knowledge and experience, what do you think the level of qualification of the Key Person should be?

What knowledge and skills do you think they need, especially in relation to attachment, child abuse and ACEs?

Is this knowledge and understanding different depending on the age group of the child?

Rose and Rogers (2012) put forward a model for understanding the multi-layered role for adults in ECEC settings. Drawing on the experiences of their Early Childhood students, they developed the notion of the 'plural practitioner'. This reflected that different times and different children required different things of them (see Table 8.3).

Table 8.3: The seven dimensions of the plural practitioner

Overview	
Critical reflector	The individual working in ECEC needs to understand their own belief systems as well as critique research and practice to promote child-centred practice based on social justice.
Carer	This is of central importance with all work with children: the actual need to 'care' for them and provide a nurturing, empathetic relationship, treating children with kindness and respect. This is not about working with children being 'women's work': we all need someone holding us in mind. In relation to attachment, it is the notion of 'mind-mindfulness' (see Chapter 3).
Communicator	Infants and young children need adults who are able to communicate and listen to what they say, verbally and non-verbally. Those working in ECEC also need to communicate orally and in writing to parents and carers and other professionals, as well as being skilled in forming relationships.
Facilitator	Here, the adult in the setting is working alongside children, empowering and 'promoting their autonomy, imagination, decision-making, and problem solving capacities' (Rose and Rogers 2012, p.68). For children who experience early trauma, it is important to constantly provide opportunities for these skills to be developed.

Overview

Observer	Having a range of observational assessment techniques that empower planning and start with the child is important in promoting their development. There are statutory requirements for observations for planning, but they need to be purposeful in enabling the child's development rather than being undertaken just for compliance.
Assessor	Observations need to inform assessment and understanding of the child. In other words, what are the observations telling us about the child, their interests, how they learn and their wider needs?
Creator	Rose and Rogers use the term 'creator' rather than 'planner' to reinforce the importance of creativity in developing empowering environments that are enabling and that meet the diverse needs of children and capture their imagination.

Source: Based on Rose and Rogers (2012)

Reflection point

Do you think these dimensions are right?

What do you think is involved in each area?

CASE STUDY: CHRISTOPHER

Christopher has just celebrated his third birthday. He was born prematurely at seven months gestation, and had to be weaned off drugs. He spent the first four months of his life in a high dependency unit in a hospital, and now has speech delay and some difficulties with coordination. The health visitor is concerned that he is small for his age and underweight; he has sallow skin colouring and his hair is dull and thin.

He was originally in the care of his mother, but there were concerns about abuse and neglect – she seemed unable to meet his needs. He was received into care when he was 18 months old and spent six months in a foster home. During this time his mother had intensive support, stopped taking drugs and Christopher was returned to her care when he was two years old.

More recently Christopher was found to have bruising, and an Emergency Protection Order was sought to remove him from his mother's care. He is currently in a foster home with the view that the local authority will apply for a Care Order. The care plan is that he will be placed for adoption.

Christopher started attending the setting when he was two years old, originally for 15 hours per week, and is now there for 30 hours, six hours a day. He has had two different Key Workers during this time, although he tends to gravitate to another member of staff who is a similar size and colouring to his mother.

His behaviour is erratic: sometimes he is quiet and withdrawn, and other times he is overly active and unable to concentrate on any activities. He also always seems hungry and can often be found near the snack area; he cries for no reason and sometimes hits other children or tries to take what they are playing with. When he is able to engage in activities, he enjoys lining things up and organising things, running and trying to jump, activities that suggest his schema for learning is 'trajectory' (Roberts 2006).

Exercise: Addressing a child's holistic development
Using the Unique Childhoods Model as a framework, consider how the setting can address Christopher's holistic development.

Values
- How is the ethos of the setting embedded in practice?
- How are visitors welcomed?
- How does the setting embrace children and families from diverse backgrounds?
- How do the values reflect that Christopher's needs are paramount in the setting?

Pedagogy
Using the 'characteristics of effective learning' and 'areas of learning and development' (see Table 8.2), how:
- Is Christopher's personal, social and emotional development including his health, wellbeing and the development of his resilience as well as his early learning, being addressed?
- Are observations being used to inform planning to address his care and learning needs?
- Is the characteristic of effective learning being used to ensure he has the foundations for later learning?
- Is his work being documented as a record for him in the future and to be given to his mother?
- Are observations being recorded to support the information being provided for the care proceedings?
- Are the foster carers being engaged and involved?

Leadership
- How are those leading the setting supporting all staff with this complex situation?
- How are they ensuring that Christopher's needs are being addressed?
- How is supervision being used?

Staff

- Using the dimensions of the plural practitioner, how would Christopher's Key Person promote his development?
- What knowledge and skills do you think staff require?
- What training or support should be provided?
- How can supervision be used?
- What professionals is the setting working with? For example, a health visitor, paediatrician and speech and language therapist.

Progress

- How is Christopher's progress being measured and recorded?
- How is this being shared with the relevant professionals?

Research

- How is research about the influence of drugs during pregnancy, premature birth, child abuse, attachment and brain development being used to support the pedagogical approaches?

Budget

- How is the budget being used to meet his needs? For example, in England the Early Years Pupil Premium.

Compliance

- How are all the compliance issues for child protection procedures, sharing information and working with others being fulfilled?
- How has this model enabled you to reflect on Christopher's holistic needs?
- Are any areas missing?

Christopher requires an environment and practitioners and professionals working alongside him who value him in his own right, a setting where the ethos evidences respectful, nurturing care and recognises the importance of sensitive communication. The setting should also reflect an understanding of the complex and diverse needs and experiences of children and their families. Adults working alongside Christopher do not need to know everything about his life, but they need to be aware of how trauma and other adverse life experiences influence all aspects of development. He needs a Key Person but also needs to be supported in developing attachments with other adults in the setting in case his Key Person is on leave, off sick, or decides to leave their employment or is not available because they are attending a meeting or have other demands on their time.

Those leading the setting or who have the specific information about his background have a responsibility to ensure Christopher is being provided with nurturing opportunities that promote his health, wellbeing and overall development, especially his language, and early learning. Children respond to abuse and separation differently, and their behaviour can change dramatically over a day. Observations should be used to understand 'trigger points' that may lead him to be distressed or influence his behaviour. Time needs to be spent settling him into the day, and planning should start with how he is when he arrives. He may need time spent with him soothing him if he is in a state of high arousal and then engaging him in deciding what he would like to do. Furthermore, through developing a deep understanding of his needs, Christopher will need opportunities for rich language development as well as developing his fine and gross motor skills. Christopher also requires activities that enable him to understand about feelings and emotions as well as cause and effect and how to develop resilience, in other words, the skills discussed earlier in this chapter that will support him to:

- Manage adversity
- Promote his self-efficacy

- Understand the difference between right and wrong
- Express how he feels.

His health needs must also be considered including that snacks and lunches reflect his requirements for a balanced diet and enable him to understand when he is hungry or full. He will also need opportunities to ensure he accesses the outside to support Vitamin D production.

Christopher may require specific resources, for example, one-to-one support, and staff may require specific training in, for example, how premature birth and drugs can affect development, techniques for working with delayed speech, and skills in working with foster carers and other professionals. To maintain his confidentiality this should be whole-setting training. It is also important that those working alongside him are supervised and that information is recorded appropriately, both for him in the future and to be shared with other professionals. This information needs to reflect his progress and/or the barriers to learning he is experiencing.

Practice point: Starting with the child

This section has purposefully not given specific activities to follow, and there is no magic list to use; rather, it is about how you *apply* knowledge and use your skills to observe, assess, plan and, most importantly, care for and nurture infants and young children. Those who have experienced abuse or who live in adverse environments need everything that all children need, but in ways that ensure they feel safe in the setting, emotionally and psychologically as well as physically.

The adults responsible for the day-to-day care and learning of individual children must be attuned to the children's needs. They should have an ongoing *virtual suitcase of practice* of creative ideas and practices to draw on. The children require adults who are consistent and

---

predictable, ensuring they do what they say they will. Routines are also important, and children need to be held in mind at every level of the setting.

Planning must start with how the children are when they come into the setting. It is important to remember that no one learns when they are distressed, and time must be taken to sooth and calm them so they can engage in the opportunities the setting provides. For young children, it is the care, warmth, nurturing and consistent responses they receive when they are aroused that support attachment, self-regulation and a sense of self. Any opportunity that supports attachment opportunities should be relished and maximised to the full – children should never be left to cry, for example.

Children need to receive praise for even the smallest things they achieve, and have places where they can take 'time out'. Large bean bags in settings are invaluable, as is supporting children to breathe properly. Any transition they have must be handled sensitively and with care. It is also important to remember that adults find it hard to articulate why they feel the way they do, and for children this is even harder. Moreover, children have the right to feel angry, sad and confused about the situation they are in. They need adults in the setting who appreciate this, and that sometimes you just need to be 'in the moment', with no words, no activities, just acknowledging quietly, verbally or non-verbally, how the child is.

Those leading the setting should ensure that it is responsive to the diverse needs of the children and their families. They also need to ensure that training opportunities are available and the appropriate support and supervision is provided to reflect on and enhance practice. Additionally, every individual in the setting should recognise their own responsibility for training and continuing professional development.

Safe practice

Previous chapters have addressed the policy and procedures relating to safe recruitment, the recognition and reporting of suspected abuse and whistleblowing, as well as the legal responsibility to share information. This section is about you and your responsibility to ensure you have the knowledge and skills to be a 'safe' practitioner and to create the right environments for children. The discussion uses the Unique Childhoods Model as a method of addressing your own developmental needs throughout your career.

First, it is important to revisit the issues raised in the Introduction about how your own experiences, both as a child and in your relationships with others, could affect your professional work. There will also be times when you are facing challenges in your private life that may influence your work with children. Examples here include a bereavement, separation, divorce, redundancy or financial difficulties. The most important issue here is that everyone faces challenges, and that you are able to address them effectively and seek support if necessary. Here I want to introduce you to a training model used in continental Europe for those who are *social pedagogues* to differentiate between the professional, personal and private dimensions in interactions with children.

The social pedagogue works with the whole child and supports their all-round development. There are different types of pedagogues, including those who specifically focus on working alongside a child who has been abused. Parents are often referred to as the first pedagogues, being recognised and valued as the first educators in the broadest sense of their children. In fact, pedagogy is about 'education' in the broadest sense of that word. The study of Early Childhood in the UK has synergy with the training of the pedagogue, and in some parts of the UK specific degree and training courses have developed. In England, the Early Years Teacher (0–5) and his or her predecessor, the Early Years

Professional, are more akin to the social pedagogue than the traditional 'teacher'.

Children's rights and participation are central to the work of the social pedagogue. Theory, professional knowledge and creative and practical skills inform their work with groups and individuals. The social pedagogue recognises that working with children requires skills in working with uncertainty and therefore, in dialogue with colleagues, constantly reviews situations and decisions. This reflective approach is vital in work with children, especially those living in challenging circumstances. Planning needs to be flexible, starting with how the child presents on the day rather than any formalised rigid planning they have to fit into (Cameron 2007; Hatton 2013; Kornbeck and Lumsden 2009; Petrie *et al.* 2006).

It is the interrelationship between the 'professional', 'personal' and 'private' (the '3 Ps') that has an important place in the training and work of the pedagogue. Bengtsson *et al.* (2008, p.9) argued that the '3 Ps' enable you to '...interact with a child or young person, build a relationship with the young person, be a role model and be authentic'. This model has much to offer those working in Early Childhood to develop 'safe' practice with children that is 'authentic'.

Practice point: The private, personal and professional

The private pedagogue is: '...the person who is known to your friends and family. The private pedagogue should not be in any relationship with a child in care. The private pedagogue is who you are outside your work' (Bengtsson *et al.* 2008, p.9).

The personal pedagogue is: '...who you are within the professional setting. This is where you use "yourself". The personal P is what you offer to the [child] young person. If you want to build a relation with a young person, you have

---

CREATING THE RIGHT ENVIRONMENT

to put yourself into the relationship so the [child] young person can relate to you' (Bengtsson *et al.* 2008, p.10).

The professional pedagogue brings knowledge and understanding together to make sense of what is happening. It provides the framework to ensure that our private self is protected. The professional pedagogue reflects on their own practice and that of others, as well as evaluating the progress being made (Bengtsson *et al.* 2008).

What does this mean in practice?

The 3 Ps offers a framework to understand the relationship between our work, our 'inner' self and what we bring of ourselves to work. Simply put, the children we work alongside need individuals who actively use reflection to understand their actions and those of others, professionals who understand how their authentic self supports their work and ensure their 'private self' does not affect their work. When issues in our private lives do begin to impact on their professional work, we should be able to recognise if we require supervision, other support or time off. Sometimes, others need to enable us to recognise this.

In other words, those we work alongside should feel safe and secure emotionally and psychologically when they are with us. They need to believe that those working with them know what they are doing, that they are 'authentic' and safe practitioners. Children and their families do not need to know the 'private you' or the issues in your own life, even though sometimes they will try to find out. Events in our own lives inform the person we are and may form the motivations for what we do, but the children we work alongside do not, and should not, know what these are.

Reflection point
What do you think of the 3 Ps model?

Think about an experience you have had at work or elsewhere where something happened that triggered emotions in you that may have made it difficult for you to work effectively. Would this model have enabled you to understand what was happening?

When training as a social worker I was shadowing a colleague whose partner was ill. On a home visit, this was shared in full with the family. This experience was back in 1983 but still informs my own professional practice. The family needed assistance with their issue, not the social worker's issue.

What the 3 Ps model does is provide a framework to monitor our own 'safe' practice. Our professional role is to ensure it is the needs of children and families at the fore of our work, not events happening in our private lives.

While the 3 Ps provides a model for how we work, we also need to be responsible for our own continuing professional development. Those working with children choose to do so, and this choice comes with the responsibility for ongoing professional development.

Exercise: Professional self
Using the Unique Childhoods Model, think about your values, your aspiration for your professional career, what knowledge you have and what your current developmental needs are.

Values

- What are your values?
- What has informed these?
- How are these evident in your work and relationships with others?

Pedagogy

- What is the philosophy underpinning your pedagogical approaches?
- Can you articulate this in writing and orally to others?
- How have your experiences influenced you?
- What are your current developmental needs in this area?

Leadership

- What do you know about leadership and management theory and practice?
- How do you lead others?
- How do you role model to others?
- How do you work alongside children to enable them to lead on their learning?
- What are your current training needs?

Staff

- What is your role in teams?
- Does your role vary in different teams or groups you are part of?
- How do you relate to your colleagues and other professionals?
- What skills do you have in collaborative working?
- What areas do you need to develop?

Progress

- How do you measure your progress?

- What specific measures do you put in place to plan your professional development, assess your ongoing needs and implement achievable targets?
- If you are involved in performance development, how do you use this to develop your practice?

Research

- What do you think the role of research has in your professional development and practice?
- How do you keep yourself up to date?
- How do you share research with those you work with?

Budget

- What actions do you take to understand funding issues?

Compliance

- How do you ensure you are compliant with all the legislative and statutory requirements you have to meet?
- Do you proactively engage in the relevant training or see it as a 'tick box' exercise?
- How do you extend your knowledge and understanding in these areas?

Have you been able to answer all these questions?

How do you think this model can help shape and articulate your professional self and your ongoing developmental needs?

How do you think maintaining a clear focus on your own professional development promotes high-quality ECEC environments that address the safeguarding and welfare of all children?

Chapter summary

This chapter has highlighted the importance of creating ECEC environments that are responsive, sensitive and attuned to the unique needs of individual infants and young children. The Unique Childhoods Model has provided a flexible framework to support you to 'make sense' of ECEC provision and practice and your own responsibility to be a safe practitioner. Most importantly, there is a clear message that there are no quick answers for children who have experienced abuse or who are living in adverse home environments. It is our responsibility, individually and collectively, to ensure that knowledge, research and practice wisdom is *applied* to ECEC and starts with the child.

Key learning

- Infants and young children respond differently to their experiences, and their behaviour can manifest itself in a variety of ways at different times of the day.
- There are no set answers or lists of what to do. What is important is to apply knowledge, research and practice wisdom to professional practice that has the child, their strengths and their holistic development needs at the centre.
- Children experiencing adversity need attuned, sensitive ECEC that is responsive and holds them in mind in every dimension of the setting's work.
- Strong professional leadership is needed that ensures that those working alongside children have the right skills and knowledge for the children they are responsible for.
- The number of children a Key Person has responsibility for must reflect the children's needs rather than the constraints of staffing.

- Additional funding, such as the Early Years Pupil Premium, must be used effectively to support the Key Person role in this crucial area.
- Adults working in ECEC have a responsibility for their own continuing professional development.
- They need to ensure they are safe reliable practitioners who know what they are doing.
- Supervision should support practitioners and professionals to develop their practice and ensure their own private issues are not brought into their direct work with children *and their families.*

Useful resources

For advice and guidance
Center on the Developing Child, https://developingchild. harvard.edu/science/key-concepts/resilience. This provides invaluable information on developing resilience in children.

Curriculum frameworks
England, Foundation Years, www.foundationyears.org.uk. This web page provides information on the EYFS.

Scotland, https://beta.gov.scot/policies/early-education-and-care. This web page provides a portal to find out about the Early Years framework in Scotland.

Wales, http://gov.wales/topics/educationandskills/foundation-phase/?lang=en and http://gov.wales/topics/people-and-communities/people/children-and-young-people/early-years/?lang=en. These web pages provide information on Foundation Phase 3–7 and the approach to Early Years 0–7.

Northern Ireland, www.education-ni.gov.uk/articles/early-years-education. This web page provides information on the Early Years curriculum.

Further reading

Mitchell, E. (2014) 'Curricula and Pedagogic Principles in the Foundation Stage (0–5).' In P. Mukherji and L. Dryden (eds) *Foundations of Early Childhood: Principles and Practice*. London: Sage, pp.225–243. This chapter introduces the underpinning principles of curriculum and pedagogy.

Johnson, T. (2016) 'Holistic Development: The Social and Emotional needs of Children.' In L. Trodd (ed.) *The Early Years Handbook for Students and Practitioners: An Essential Guide for the Foundation Degree Levels 4 and 5*. Abingdon: Routledge. pp.231–245. This chapter in this really useful text explores the social and emotional needs of infants and young children. It also addresses the role of the Key Person and has a strong emphasis on reflective practice.

Murray, J. (2017) *Building Knowledge in Early Childhood Education: Young Children Are Researchers*. Abingdon: Routledge. This book provides plentiful examples of how to enable young children to construct their own knowledge through their research activities.

Rose, J. and Rogers. S. (2012) *The Role of the Adult in Early Years Settings*. Maidenhead: Open University Press. This book addresses the different roles of those working in ECEC and the importance of a child centred approach.

Roberts, R. (2011) *Well-being from Birth*. London: Sage. The main focus of this book is on how adults can promote the wellbeing of young children. It provides both theoretical perspectives and practice examples.

Chapter 9

Reflecting on Learning and Practice

Chapter objectives

By the end of this chapter you will be able to:
- Identify key learning about child protection
- Describe your own role in working alongside children who are experiencing or have experienced early trauma
- Recognise your ongoing learning requirements
- Explain the challenges inherent in the safeguarding of children.

Introduction

The real strength of studying Early Childhood for those working in ECEC is the opportunity it affords to develop inter-disciplinary knowledge and skills to apply to practice. However, as this book has emphasised, this learning is not a one-off event – it is a lifelong journey. Indeed, the more you learn, the more you appreciate the areas you still need to understand. In the preparation and crafting of this book, my own learning journey has been immense. This journey has reinforced my belief that the professionalisation of the ECEC workforce in the UK brings opportunities to create a new script for infants and young children living with early trauma, in adverse environments and experiencing disadvantage. However, findings from successive SCRs and the emphasis on inspection regimes appear to have led to a greater focus on process rather than practice. Moreover, as Ferguson (2017) rightly articulated, the child can become invisible in this process.

This book has sought to rebalance this, encouraging new ways of thinking alongside an appreciation of the crucial importance of graduate leadership in ECEC. Each chapter has aimed to provide the architecture for you to build on throughout your career. This chapter specifically draws together key points about the role of ECEC in child protection. It considers the importance of graduate leadership, the application of theory to practice and the role of ongoing learning for your continuing professional development. Finally, it looks to the future and the actions needed to really change the script for those infants and young children who need protecting.

Importance of ECEC for child protection

Each chapter of this book should have contributed to your understanding about the important role of ECEC in the field of child protection. As previous discussion in the book has emphasised, sustained contact with infants and young children, the majority of whom have not been abused, brings insights that other agencies may not have, for example, knowledge about who is actually caring for the child, if there has been a change of partner, a new pregnancy and whether the family has moved address. These insights contribute to the early identification and intervention in cases where a child is at risk of significant harm or has been abused. They also support planning and the wider inter-agency assessment processes. Chapter 8 identified that those working in ECEC cannot directly change home environments, although they can provide high-quality setting experiences for young children underpinned by sensitive, attuned, nurturing care that offers a window for change, an environment where those working within it appreciate the unique needs of each child and understand the importance of attachment behaviours (see also Chapter 4).

Creating the right environment for infants and young children attending ECEC is imperative, and the Unique Childhoods Model has been presented as a flexible framework to analyse, critique and reflect on practice, a model that promotes a strengths approach to all aspects of our work. Not all infants and young children 'in need' attend ECEC, but for those who do, using a strengths approach that focuses on enhancing the child's capacity to learn, develop new skills and resilience can lead to change. To achieve this, there are some core principles that are applicable to practice in ECEC across the UK:

- Children's needs must be paramount in all we do.
- Early detection and intervention are crucial.
- ECEC environments should recognise the uniqueness of every child and provide safe, nurturing care and enabling environments that keep infants and young children safe and promote wellbeing and healthy development.
- Parents and caregivers have an important role to play, and should be engaged in understanding their child's developmental and early learning needs.
- Staff must understand the role of policy and procedures and the need to follow them. This includes raising concerns about the practice in the setting and adults working there.
- Adults working in ECEC must be able to recognise the signs of all types of abuse and understand the impact of living in adverse environments.
- Sharing information and working in partnership with other agencies and professionals is the responsibility of all adults working in ECEC.

- Graduate leadership is an essential ingredient to enhance practice in the area of child protection.
- Professionals and practitioners must take responsibility for their own continuing professional development.
- Supervision must be used proactively to promote reflection and personal and professional development.
- The role of training and continuing professional development is in building a workforce of reflective professionals and practitioners who recognise their role in child protection and the need to be 'safe practitioners'.

Reflection point

Do you agree with these core principles?

Would you add any?

Advocating for young children

Practice point: Giving children a voice

With an increasing focus on driving up educational attainment, reducing the disadvantage gap and the notion of 'school readiness', the voice of infants and young children can often appear invisible in debates. Consequently, it is important that those working in ECEC and the wider academic field of Early Childhood act as advocates. Furthermore, with an increasing focus on attainment, children can be categorised when they start school as, for example, not having the right level of language and communication skills, having impaired physical development, poor literacy or issues with their personal, social and emotional development (Family and Childcare Trust and NAHT 2017; Ofsted 2016).

The importance and value of these areas of development cannot be underestimated. The crucial point here is that young children learn and develop at different rates, and their ability to learn is influenced by their health, wellbeing and the environments in which they live. Indeed, there are multiple influences on early development that make it immensely difficult to reduce the disadvantage gap. These include:

- Challenges in identifying infants and young children experiencing adverse home environments.
- Events in the first 1001 days, from conception to the age of two. These can adversely affect the development of the brain's architecture and the attachment of infants with their primary caregivers.
- Not all children who are abused or who are living with the broad range of adverse life experiences are known to the authorities.
- For children who are abused, there are normally other contributing factors such as domestic violence, mental health issues or drug or alcohol misuse.
- Children who are in constant 'flight or fight' situations have raised stress hormone levels that impact on their physiology.
- There is no requirement for children under the age of five to access ECEC.
- There is a lack of a cohesive approach at policy level, with frequent policy changes and no specific government minister who has an overview of what is happening across departments. Child maltreatment requires health, especially public health, the police, housing, ECEC and education departmens to work more effectively together.
- Wherever possible, the State does not want to intervene in family life unless it has to. Even when

> abuse has occurred, children should remain in their family of origin, with appropriate services and court orders only made if there is no alternative.

Role of graduate leadership

Growing research evidence about holistic development in early childhood, especially very early childhood, reinforces the importance of graduate leadership in ECEC. Those working with infants and young children require higher-level knowledge and skills so that they can critique and apply their learning at every level of practice. They need to lead the development of others, especially in the area of safeguarding, child protection, promoting health and wellbeing, and ensuring infants and young children have skills on which to build.

In the area of child protection, settings need to reflect on the ongoing training needs of the staff and the qualification level of the designated person. In England, the Early Years Teacher (0–5) has standards to meet in relation to safeguarding and working with others, yet they do not, as a matter of course, lead in this area.

Importance of academic study and training

Infants and young children can spend long periods of time in ECEC settings, and their complex and changing needs should be paramount at all times. They do not choose the setting they attend, nor the adults charged with their early learning and care. Therefore, they have a right to a professionalised Early Years workforce that addresses inequality and 'promote[s] all aspects of children's care, health, development and learning' (Lumsden 2014, p.301). This becomes more magnified in the area of child abuse, where the exact number of children being abused or living in adverse life experiences is not known. Consequently, those working in the sector need to be able to apply theory to practice, as discussed later in this chapter.

Recruiting and maintaining staff in group care is challenging, and the number of childminders has declined (Ofsted 2017). Given this situation, strong graduate leadership is even more important. However, there is still a long way to go as the majority of those working in ECEC are qualified at Levels 2 or 3. Those leading and managing settings have a minimum qualification of Level 3. While the sector requires people at all levels, infants and young children with complex families require professionals and practitioners with relevant knowledge and skills. They require adults who:

- Are attuned to and proactively address their care and learning needs
- Can critique and analyse information
- Recognise and value the importance of keeping up to date with research
- Apply their learning to their practice and that of others.

In England, the Early Years Teacher (0–5) has a key role in this, and the requirement in the EYFS for supervision is an important vehicle for enabling reflection and personal growth and development.

Applying theory to practice

A central message in this book is that there are no quick answers to addressing child maltreatment or to changing home environments. Each case, child and family is unique, and child abuse must be understood in the wider societal context as well as at the community and individual level. Therefore, using theory to facilitate learning and to encourage new ways of thinking and practice is a vital component of your ongoing development. As discussed in the Introduction, the work of Bronfenbrenner and the development of his original theory to embrace the effect of time (chronosystem) and specific events (chaotic-system) on development has underpinned this book. It is a theoretical framework that I have always found useful in trying to 'make sense' of what is happening and what leads some people to harm the children they should be keeping safe. It also influenced the Unique Childhoods Model presented in Chapter 8, which provides a systematic model for understanding and strengthening practice in ECEC.

Reflection point

Using the work of Bronfenbrenner, reflect on your learning throughout this book. How does it promote understanding in the following areas:

- The wider influences of how policy at a national level (*macrosystem*) influences work at a local level (*exosystem*) with the family when there is suspected or actual abuse (*microsystem*).
- The effect of one-off events such as a child's death from maltreatment or incidents such as the Little Ted's Inquiry (discussed in Chapter 2) into the sexual abuse of children in ECEC on policy at a national, local and setting level (*chaotic-system*).
- Changes in what is classified as abuse over time (*chronosystem*).
- The effect of child maltreatment and living in adverse experiences over the life course (*chronosystem*).
- The importance of training and continuing professional development to improve ECEC practice at a setting level (*microsystem/mesosystem*).
- Focused work with individual children and their families (*microsystem/mesosystem*).

For those studying Early Childhood, the skills requiring development include the ability to:

- Understand that personal and professional development is an ongoing process
- Critique and analyse theory and research
- Apply learning to practice
- Reflect in and on practice
- Use supervision effectively to enhance understanding and development
- Recognise when further training or higher level learning is required.

In relation to child protection, professionals and practitioners working in ECEC should have the appropriate knowledge and skills to identify situations where a child may have been abused or is in danger of being harmed. They also need to apply their knowledge to each unique child, and work alongside them to enhance their holistic development. However, as previously discussed, there are no set approaches to this area of work: what works in one situation may not in another.

Practice point: Applying learning to practice

As discussed elsewhere, the exact circumstances of infants and children are not always known. Even when agencies are involved, no one knows exactly what the child is experiencing in the home environment. For those attending ECEC, this is where the skill of applying theory to practice is crucial. Infants and young children need to have learning opportunities that are focused on laying down the foundations for their next steps. These include language and communication, personal, social and emotional development and opportunities to enhance their physical development.

Working with the parents and caregivers so that they understand the importance of these areas for their children is important, but not always easy. Moreover, as our knowledge of early development and the impact of adverse environments grows, so does the importance of enabling parents and caregivers to appreciate how their home environment may be affecting the child's development and future learning.

Chapter 8 presented the idea of a virtual suitcase of practice. The suitcase will grow as your career progresses and as you gain more knowledge and experience. We never stop learning from reflecting on our own practice and from our colleagues. The virtual suitcase will also contain ideas for working with children, offering you choices to draw on if one approach doesn't work. However, the important thing for you to note is that you are in charge of this suitcase. It is your responsibility to continue to learn, and in turn, it is your responsibility to share your learning and knowledge with others. In summary, the most important item packed in your suitcase is you – a reflective professional who has social justice for children at your heart and that you know what you will and will not compromise on.

Three important items in my virtual suitcase are the lessons I have learned from colleagues and practice:

- Always be authentic in your work and have the confidence to be 'you'. I learnt very quickly that copying exactly how a colleague I valued practised did not work. The skill is to observe, learn and then apply to your own practice.
- The importance of *'greeting someone at the station'* with kindness, a smile and ensuring they know what they have to do and where they have to go. We all know what it is like to be somewhere we do not know and how lovely it is to be welcomed, shown where everything is and given a drink.

In short, ensure you practise with empathy, kindness and 'mind-mindedness' for others (see Chapter 3).

· In working alongside adults, children and young people who may have abused others, always ensure that you are objective and look beyond the behaviour to the causes. This does not mean that you condone the behaviour; rather, try and understand the reasons that led to the actions and work towards preventing it happening again (see Chapter 4).

Reflection point

Make a list of what you already have in your virtual suitcase.

Decide on the three items that are most important to you, and reflect on how they enhance your practice.

How do you 'greet people at the station'?

Looking to the future

There have been substantial changes in ECEC over the last two decades, including the growth of Early Childhood as an academic discipline and specific practitioner and graduate professional roles. These changes afford ECEC a unique opportunity to make a difference to the short-, medium- and long-term outcomes of infants and young children. Those working in the sector increasingly have the inter-disciplinary knowledge and skills in early learning and care that should enhance their practice. They must, however, as this book has repeatedly stressed, recognise their individual responsibility for changing practice, as well as for their own continuing professional development and applying research to practice.

For those who attend ECEC settings, there are abundant opportunities to forge strong foundations. However, the real challenge is ensuring that compliance does not outweigh the importance of an Early Years pedagogy that has nurturing, sensitive, attuned care and the safeguarding and welfare of all children at its core. As Chapter 3 illustrated, the causes of child abuse are not just at an individual level; they are multifaceted and have structural, cultural and institutional dimensions. With an increasingly complex and diverse society, ECEC offers a window of change, a chance to proactively shape a different future. Those working in ECEC are accountable for the services they provide and must ensure they fulfil their responsibility to create environments that promote high-quality nurturing care and early learning experiences. However, real change for those infants and young children being abused and living in adverse environments will only happen when policy really embraces research, recognises the 'very' Early Years period and there is financial investment that is longer than the period of one government.

With increasing public health intelligence, the ongoing need for a holistic approach at every level of society to assist and intervene in family life throughout the life cycle is now an essential requirement for future planning. As Pringle and Naidoo (1975, p.169) articulated so well, we have to break '...the vicious circle of the emotional or intellectually deprived children of today becoming tomorrow's parents of yet another generation of deprived children'. The children they were talking about are today's parents and grandparents of yet another generation who have been abused.

The message here is clear – history shows us how hard it is to change the inter-generational cycle of abuse and disadvantage, but this should not stop us. As I have argued throughout this book, the development of Early Childhood as an academic discipline and the professionalisation of the ECEC workforce provide new opportunities to change the script for those children experiencing adversity, now and in the future. The growing inter-disciplinary knowledge and research base about the holistic development of infants and young children provide crucial opportunities for change. These must be grasped and we must learn from history.

Finally, those studying and working in ECEC must take every opportunity to *advocate* for the developmental needs of infants and young children. If they are not valued as citizens with rights, who need protection, love and nurturing, as well as safe adults and environments, the disadvantage gap will continue to grow. For those facing the worse trauma of all, abuse by those who are meant to love and nurture them, the impact lasts beyond their lifetime, affecting not only the individual, but future generations and society as well.

References

Adoption and Children Act (2002) London: HMSO. Accessed on 10/10/17 at
www.legislation.gov.uk/ukpga/2002/38/contents

Ainsworth, M., Blehar, M., Walters, W. and Wall, S. (2015) *Patterns of
Attachment: A Psychological Study of the Strange Situation* (Psychology
Press & Routledge Classic Editions). Hove: Psychology Press. [Original
work published 1978.]

Anning, A., Cottrell, D., Frost, N., Green, J. and Robinson, M. (2010)
Developing Multi-professional Teamwork for Integrated Children's Services
(2nd edn). Maidenhead: Open University Press.

APPG (All-Party Parliamentary Group) on FASD (Foetal Alcohol Spectrum
Disorders) (2015) *Initial Report of the Inquiry into the Current Picture of
FASD in the UK today*. Accessed on 7/4/17 at www.appg-fasd.org.uk/
reports/4589489444

APPG Conception to Age 2 (2015) *Building Great Britons*. Accessed on 10/4/17
at https://plct.files.wordpress.com/2012/11/building-great-britons-
report-conception-to-age-2-feb-2015.pdf

Balbernie, R. (2013) 'The importance of secure attachment for infant
mental health.' *Journal of Health Visiting 1*, 210–217. Accessed on 26/4/17
at www.journalofhealthvisiting.com/cgi-bin/go.pl/library/article.
cgi?uid=98131;article=hv_1_4_210_217

Balbernie, R. (2015) 'Security and Attachment.' In M. Reed and R. Walker (eds) *Early Childhood*. London: Sage, pp.131–141.

Balbernie, R. (2017) 'Hazards and hopes in the early years.' *International Journal of Birth and Parent Education 5*, 1, 5–8.

Barlow, J. (2017) 'AIMH UK Best Practice Guidance (BPG) No 4: The relationship with the unborn baby: Why it matters.' *International Journal of Birth and Parent Education 5*, 1.

Barlow, J., SchraderMillan, A., Axford, N., Wrigley, Z., Sonthalia, S., Wilkinson, T., *et al.* (2015) 'Attachment and attachment-related outcomes in pre-school children: A review of recent evidence.' *Child and Adolescent Mental Health 12138*, 1–10.

BASW (British Association of Social Workers) (2017) 'Social Work Careers.' Accessed on 29/9/17 at www.basw.co.uk/social-work-careers/#whatissocialwork

Beckett, C. (2007) *Child Protection: An Introduction* (2nd edn). London: Sage.

Bellis, A.M., Lowey, H., Leckenby, N., Hughes, K. and Harrison, D. (2014) 'Adverse childhood experiences: Retrospective study to determine their impact on adult health behaviours and health outcomes in a UK population.' *Journal of Public Health (Oxford) 36*, 1, 81–91.

Bengtsson, E., Chamberlain, C., Crimmens, D. and Stanley, J. (2008) *Introducing Social Pedagogy into Residential Child Care in England: An Evaluation of a Project. Social Education Trust.* Accessed on 4/4/17 at www.childrenwebmag.com/wp-content/uploads/2008/03/introducing-sp-into-rcc-in-england-final-reportfeb2008.pdf

Bentley, H., O'Hagan, O., Raff, A., Bhatti, I. and Reid, C. (2016) *How Safe Are Our Children? The Most Comprehensive Overview of Child Protection in the UK 2016.* London: NSPCC. Accessed on 21/10/17 at www.nspcc.org.uk/services-and-resources/research-and-resources/2016/how-safe-are-our-children-2016

Bernard, C. and Harris, P. (2016) *Safeguarding Black Children: Good Practice in Child Protection.* London: Jessica Kingsley Publishers.

Black, M., Walker, S., Fernald, L., Andersen, C., Digirolamo, A., Chunling, L., *et al.* (2017) 'Early childhood development coming of age: Science through the life course.' *Lancet 389*, 77–90. Accessed on 10/11/17 at www.thelancet.com/pdfs/journals/lancet/PIIS0140-6736%2816%2931389-7.pdf

Bournemouth University (2017) *Simulated Child Protection Conference.* Accessed 04/01/18 at https://www.youtube.com/watch?v=x1Z-zJDWrjI

Bowlby, J. (1955) *Maternal Care and Mental Health.* World Health Organization Monograph (No 2). Accessed on 28/4/17 at http://darkwing.uoregon.edu/~eherman/teaching/texts/Bowlby%20Maternal%20Care%20and%20Mental%20Health.pdf

Bowlby, J. (1969) *Attachment and Loss.* London: Hogarth Press.

Bowlby, J. (1988) *A Secure Base.* New York: Basic Books.

Bowlby, R. (2007) 'Babies and toddlers in non-parental daycare can avoid stress and anxiety if they develop a lasting secondary attachment bond with one carer who is consistently accessible to them.' *Attachment and Human Development 9,* 4, 307–319.

British Medical Association Board of Science (2013) *Growing Up in the UK: Ensuring a Healthy Future for Our Children.* London: British Medical Association Board of Science.

Britto, P.R., Lye, S.J., Proulx, K., Yousafzai, A.K., Matthews, S.G., Vaivada, T., *et al.* (2017) 'Nurturing care: Promoting early childhood development.' *Lancet 389,* 91–102.

Bronfenbrenner, U. (1979) *The Ecology of Human Development: Experiments by Nature and Design.* Cambridge, MA: Harvard University Press.

Bronfenbrenner, U. (1992) *Ecological Systems Theory.* London: Jessica Kingsley Publishers.

Bronfenbrenner, U. (ed.) (2005) *Making Human Beings Human: Bioecological Perspectives on Human Development.* London: Sage.

Cafcass (Children and Family Court Advisory and Support Service) (2017) 'Children's Guardian.' Accessed on 28/10/17 at www.cafcass.gov.uk/about-cafcass/care-proceedings.aspx

Calder, M., McKinnon, M. and Sneddon, R. (2012) *National Framework of Risk to Support the Assessment of Children and Young People.* Edinburgh: Scottish Government. Accessed on 8/12/17 at http://hub.careinspectorate.com/media/109497/sg-national-risk-framework-to-support-assessment.pdf

Cameron, C. (2007) 'Social pedagogy and the children's workforce.' Community Care. Accessed on 26/8/17 at www.communitycare.co.uk/2007/08/08/social-pedagogy-and-the-childrens-workforce/

Carr, H. and Goosey, D. (2017) *Law for Social Workers* (14th edn). Oxford: Oxford University Press.

Center on the Developing Child at Harvard University (2013) 'In Brief: Early Childhood Mental Health.' Cambridge, MA: Centre on the Developing Child. Accessed on 10/4/17 at http://46y5eh11fhgw3ve3ytpwxt9r. wpengine.netdna-cdn.com/wp-content/uploads/2015/05/InBrief-Early-Childhood-Mental-Health-1.pdf

Center on the Developing Child at Harvard University (2016) *From Best Practice to Breakthrough Impacts: A Science Based Approach for Building a More Promising Future for Young Children and Families.* Accessed on 04/01/18 at http://developingchild.harvard.edu/wp-content/ uploads/2016/05/From_Best_Practices_to_Breakthrough_Impacts-4. pdf

Center on the Developing Child at Harvard University (2017) '8 Things to Remember about Child Development.' Cambridge, MA: Centre on the Developing Child. Accessed on 16/4/17 at http://developingchild. harvard.edu/resources/8-things-remember-child-development/

Cherry, L. (2013) *The Brightness of Stars: Stories of Adults Who Came Through the British Care System.* Banbury: Wilson King Publishers.

Children Act (1989) London: HMSO. Accessed on 24/4/17 at www.legislation. gov.uk/ukpga/1989/41

Children (Northern Ireland) Order, The (1995) London: HMSO. Accessed on 30/10/17 at www.legislation.gov.uk/nisi/1995/755/contents/made

Children (Scotland) Act (1995) London: HMSO. Accessed on 30/10/17 at www. legislation.gov.uk/ukpga/1995/36/contents

Children and Social Work Act (2017) London: HMSO. Accessed on 24/4/17 at www.legislation.gov.uk/ukpga/2017/16/contents

Cleaver, H., Unell, I. and Aldgate, J. (2011) *Children's Needs – Parenting Capacity: Child Abuse: Parental Mental Illness, Learning Disability, Substance Misuse, and Domestic Violence* (2nd edn). Norwich: The Stationery Office. Accessed on 6/4/17 at www.gov.uk/government/uploads/system/ uploads/attachment_data/file/182095/DFE-00108-2011-Childrens_ Needs_Parenting_Capacity.pdf

College of Policing (2017) *Major Investigation and Public Protection Staffing and the Child Abuse Investigation Unit.* Accessed on 29/10/17 at www. app.college.police.uk/app-content/major-investigation-and-public-protection/managing-sexual-offenders-and-violent-offenders

Conkbayir, M. (2017) *Early Childhood and Neuroscience.* London: Bloomsbury Publishing Plc.

Corby, B. (2006) *Child Abuse: Towards a Knowledge Base* (3rd edn). Maidenhead: Open University Press.

Corby, B., Shemmings, D. and Wilkins, D. (2012) *Child Abuse: An Evidence Base for Confident Practice* (4th edn). Maidenhead: Open University Press.

Couper, S. and Mackie, P. (2016) *'Polishing the Diamonds' – Addressing Adverse Childhood Experiences in Scotland.* Glasgow: NHS Health Scottish. Accessed on 30/10/17 at www.scotphn.net/wp-content/uploads/2016/06/2016_05_26-ACE-Report-Final-AF.pdf

D'Arcy, M. and Gosling, P. (1998) *Abuse of Trust: Frank Beck and the Leicestershire Children's Homes Scandal.* London: Bowerdean Publishing Co.

DBS (Disclosure and Barring Service) (2017) 'Apply to check someone else's criminal record.' Accessed on 31/10/17 at www.gov.uk/government/organisations/disclosure-and-barring-service

DCSF (2010) *Working Together to Safeguard Children: A Guide to Inter-Agency Working to Safeguard and Promote the Welfare of Children.* London: HM Government. Accessed on 22/10/17 at www.lcitylscb.org/media/1151/working-together-2010.pdf

DfE (Department for Education) (2007) *Safeguarding Children from Abuse Linked to a Belief in Spirit Possession.* London: HM Government. Accessed on 29/1/17 at http://webarchive.nationalarchives.gov.uk/20130401151715/http://www.education.gov.uk/publications/eOrderingDownload/DFES-00465-2007.pdf

DfE (2013a) *Early Years Teachers' Standards.* London: HM Government. Accessed on 22/10/17 at www.gov.uk/government/publications/early-years-teachers-standards

DfE (2013b) *Working Together to Safeguard Children: A Guide to Inter-Agency Working to Safeguard and Promote the Welfare of Children.* London: DfE. Accessed on 15/1/17 at www.gov.uk/government/uploads/system/uploads/attachment_data/file/417669/Archived-Working_together_to_safeguard_children.pdf

DfE (2014) *Statutory Framework for the Early Years Foundation Stage: Setting the Standards for Learning Development and Care for Children from Birth to Five.* London: DfE. Accessed on 17/1/17 at www.foundationyears.org.uk/files/2017/03/EYFS_STATUTORY_FRAMEWORK_2017.pdf

DfE (2015a) *Working Together to Safeguard Children: A Guide to Inter-Agency Working to Safeguard and Promote the Welfare of Children.* London: DfE. Accessed on 15/1/17 at www.gov.uk/government/uploads/system/ uploads/attachment_data/file/417669/Archived-Working_together_to_ safeguard_children.pdf

DfE (2015b) *What to Do if You're Worried a Child is Being Abused: Advice for Practitioners.* London: HM Government. Accessed on 28/1/17 at www. gov.uk/government/uploads/system/uploads/attachment_data/ file/419604/What_to_do_if_you_re_worried_a_child_is_being_abused. pdf

DfE (2015c) *Information Sharing: Advice for Practitioners Providing Safeguarding Services to Children, Young People, Parents and Carers.* London: HMSO. Accessed on 15/1/17 at www.gov.uk/government/publications/ safeguarding-practitioners-information-sharing-advice

DfE (2016a) *Characteristics of Children in Need: 2015 to 2016.* London: DfE. Accessed on 28/1/17 at www.gov.uk/government/statistics/ characteristics-of-children-in-need-2015-to-2016

DfE (2016b) *Keeping Children Safe in Education: For Schools and Colleges.* London: DfE. Accessed on 28/1/17 at www.gov.uk/government/ publications/keeping-children-safe-in-education--2

DfE (2017a) *Statutory Framework for the Early Years Foundation Stage: Setting the Standards for Learning, Development and Care for Children from Birth to Five.* London: DfE. Accessed on 15/10/17 at www.foundationyears.org.uk/ files/2017/03/EYFS_STATUTORY_FRAMEWORK_2017.pdf

DfE (2017b) 'Get into Teaching: Become an Early Years Teacher.' London: DfE. Accessed on 15/10/17 at https://getintoteaching.education.gov.uk/ explore-my-options/become-an-early-years-teacher

DfES (Department for Education and Skills) (2004) *Children Act 2004.* London: HMSO. Accessed on 17/1/17 at www.opsi.gov.uk/acts/acts2004/ ukpga_20040031_en_1

DfES (2006) *Childcare Act 2006.* London: The Stationery Office. Accessed on 17/1/17 at www.legislation.gov.uk/ukpga/2006/21/contents

DH (Department of Health), Home Office and DfEE (Department for Education and Employment) (1999) *Working Together to Safeguard Children.* London: The Stationery Office. Accessed on 22/10/17 at http://webarchive.nationalarchives.gov.uk/20121206090835/http://www.dh.gov.uk/prod_consum_dh/groups/dh_digitalassets/@dh/@en/documents/digitalasset/dh_4075824.pdf

Direct Gov.UK (2017) *National Careers Service: School Nursing.* Accessed on 8/12/17 at https://nationalcareersservice.direct.gov.uk/job-profiles/s

Doyle, C. (2012) *Working with Abused Children: Focus on the Child* (4th edn). Basingstoke: Palgrave Macmillan.

Doyle, C. (2014) 'Protecting and Safeguarding Children.' In T. Waller and G. Davies (eds) *An Introduction to Early Childhood* (3rd edn). London: Sage, pp.223–243.

Doyle, C. and Timms, C. (2014) *Child Neglect and Emotional Abuse.* London: Sage.

Elfer, P. and Page, J. (2015) 'Pedagogy with babies: Perspectives of eight nursery managers.' *Early Child Development and Care 185,* 11–12, 1762–1782.

Fahlberg, V.I. (1991) *A Child's Journey through Placement* (UK edn). London: British Association for Adoption and Fostering (BAAF).

Family Care Trust and NAHT (National Association for Head Teachers) (2017) *School Ready Report.* Accessed on 22/10/17 at www.naht.org.uk/welcome/news-and-media/key-topics/pupil-wellbeing/school-readiness-survey/

Felitti, V.J., Anda, R.F., Nordenberg, D., Williamson, D.F., Spitz, A.M., Edwards, V., *et al.* (1998) 'Relationship of childhood abuse and household dysfunction to many of the leading causes of death in adults: The Adverse Childhood Experiences (ACE) Study.' *American Journal of Preventive Medicine 14,* 4, 245–258.

Ferguson, H. (2017) 'How children become invisible in child protection work: Findings from research into day-to-day social work practice.' *British Journal of Social Work 47,* 1007–1023.

Ford, K., Butler, N., Hughes, K., Quigg, Z. and Bellis, M.A. (2016) *Adverse Childhood Experiences (ACEs) in Hertfordshire, Luton and Northamptonshire.* Liverpool: Centre for Public Health. Accessed on 2/1/17 at www.cph.org.uk/wp-content/uploads/2016/05/Adverse-Childhood-Experiences-in-Hertfordshire-Luton-and-Northamptonshire-FINAL_compressed.pdf

Gerhardt, S. (2014) *Why Love Matters: How Affection Shapes a Baby's Brain.* Hove: Routledge.

GOV.UK (2017) 'Parental Rights and Responsibilities.' Accessed on 23/10/17 at www.gov.uk/parental-rights-responsibilities

Harker, L., Jütte, S., Murphy, T., Bentley, H., Miller, P. and Fitch, K. (2013) *How Safe Are Our Children?* Accessed on 5/4/17 at www.nspcc.org.uk/globalassets/documents/research-reports/how-safe-children-2013-report.pdf

Hatton, K. (2013) *Social Pedagogy in the UK: Theory and Practice.* Lyme Regis: Russell House Publishing Ltd.

Hazan, C. and Zeifman, D. (1994) 'Sex and the Psychological Tether.' In D. Perlman and K. Bartholomew (eds) *Advances in Personal Relationships.* London: Jessica Kingsley Publishers, pp.151–178.

Heilmann, A., Kelly, Y. and Watt, R.G. (2015) *Equally Protected? A Review of the Evidence on the Physical Punishment of Children.* Scotland: NSPCC. Accessed on 15/1/17 at www.nspcc.org.uk/globalassets/documents/research-reports/equally-protected.pdf

Herring, J. (2013) *Family Law* (6th edn). Harrow: Pearson Publications Ltd.

Herring, J. (2017) *Family Law* (8th edn). Harrow: Pearson Publications Ltd.

HM Government (2015) *Revised Prevent Duty Guidance for England and Wales.* Accessed on 24/6/17 at www.gov.uk/government/uploads/system/uploads/attachment_data/file/445977/3799_Revised_Prevent_Duty_Guidance__England_Wales_V2-Interactive.pdf

Holmes, E. (2017) 'The impact of maternal smoking in pregnancy beyond birth.' *International Journal of Birth and Parent Education 5,* 1, 13–16.

Holt, K. (2014) *Child Protection.* Basingstoke: Palgrave Macmillan.

Home Office (2016) *Domestic Violence and Abuse.* Accessed on 20/1/17 at www.gov.uk/guidance/domestic-violence-and-abuse

Howe, D. (1998) *Patterns of Attachment.* Oxford: Blackwell Science Ltd.

Howe, D. (2005) *Child Abuse and Neglect: Attachment, Development and Intervention.* Basingstoke: Palgrave Macmillan.

Hughes, D. (2006) *Building Bonds of Attachment: Awaking Love in Deeply Traumatized Children* (3rd edn). London: Rowman & Littlefield.

Human Rights Act (1998) London: HMSO. Accessed on 30/10/17 at www.legislation.gov.uk/ukpga/1998/42/contents

Humphreys, C. and Bradbury-Jones, C. (2015) 'Domestic abuse and safeguarding children: Focus, response and intervention.' *Child Abuse Review 24*, 4, 1–4.

Iwi, K. and Newman, C. (2011) *Picking Up the Pieces after Domestic Violence: A Practical Resource for Supporting Parenting Skills.* London: Jessica Kingsley Publishers.

Johnson, T. (2016) 'Holistic Development: The Social and Emotional needs of Children.' In L. Trodd (ed.) *The Early Years Handbook for Students and Practitioners: An Essential Guide for the Foundation Degree Levels 4 and 5.* Abingdon: Routledge, pp.231–245.

Joslyn, E. (2016) *Resilience in Childhood: Perspectives, Promise and Practice.* London: Palgrave.

Kay, J. (2003) *Protecting Children: A Practical Guide* (2nd edn). New York: Continuum International Publishing Group.

Kornbeck, J. and Lumsden, E. (2009) 'European Skills and Models: The Relevance of the Social Pedagogue.' In P. Higham (ed.) *Understanding Post Qualifying Social Work.* London: Sage Publications, pp.122–132.

Local Children's Safeguarding Board (LCSB) (2017) *Child Protection Conference and Plan.* Accessed on 04/01/18 at https://www.youtube.com/watch?v=YWzzcHC_9zs

Lord Laming (2003) *Inquiry into the Death of Victoria Climbié.* London: The Stationery Office.

Leadsom, A., Field, F., Burstow, P. and Lucas, C. (2013) *The 1001 Critical Days: The Importance of the Conception to Age Two Period. A Cross-Party Manifesto.* London.

Lumsden, E. (2012) 'The Early Years Professional: A New Professional or a Missed Opportunity?' PhD thesis, University of Northampton.

Lumsden, E. (2014) 'Joined-Up Thinking in Practice: An Exploration of Professional Collaboration.' In T. Waller and G. Davis (eds) *An Introduction to Early Childhood: A Multidisciplinary Approach* (3rd edn). London: Sage, pp.152–166.

Marmot, M. (2010) *Strategic Review Of Health Inequalities in England Post-2010, Fair Society, Healthy Lives: The Marmot Review.* London: Global Health Equity Group. Accessed on 8/12/17 at www.parliament.uk/documents/fair-society-healthy-lives-full-report.pdf

Marsden, F., McMahon, S. and Younde, A. (2014) 'Inter-Agency Working, Observation and Assessment.' In J. Reid and S. Burton (eds) *Safeguarding and Protecting Children in the Early Years*. Abingdon: Routledge, pp.165–179.

McKenna, Y. (2009) 'Cultural Influences on Attachment Behaviours.' A Project Submitted to the School of Graduate Studies of the University of Lethbridge in Partial Fulfilment of the Requirements for the Degree of Master of Counselling. Alberta: Faculty of Education, Lethbridge.

Moullin, S. (2017) 'Attachment: The social-emotional Basis of Scholl Readiness.' *International Journal of Birth and Parent Education 5*, 1, 17–19.

Munro, E. (2008). *Effective Child Protection* (2nd edn). London: Sage.

National Careers Service (2017a) 'School Nurse.' Accessed on 29/10/17 at https://nationalcareersservice.direct.gov.uk/job-profiles/school-nurse#

National Careers Service (2017b) 'Family Support Worker.' Accessed on 29/10/17 at https://nationalcareersservice.direct.gov.uk/job-profiles/family-support-worker

National Scientific Council on the Developing Child (2007) *The Science of Early Childhood Development: Closing the Gap Between What We Know and What We Do*. Cambridge, MA: Center on the Developing Child. Accessed on 30/10/17 at https://46y5eh11fhgw3ve3ytpwxt9r-wpengine.netdna-ssl.com/wp-content/uploads/2015/05/Science_Early_Childhood_Development.pdf

NHS (National Health Service) (2007) *Adult Psychiatric Morbidity in England – 2007: Results of a Household Survey*. Accessed on 28/10/17 at http://digital.nhs.uk/catalogue/PUB02931

NHS (2017a) 'Female Genital Mutilation (FGM).' Accessed on 29/1/17 at www.nhs.uk/conditions/female-genital-mutilation/Pages/Introduction.aspx

NHS (2017b) *Next Steps on the NHS Five Year Forward Review*. Accessed on 10/4/17 at www.england.nhs.uk/wp-content/uploads/17/03/NEXT-STEPS-ON-THE-NHS-FIVE-YEAR-FORWARD-VIEW.pdf

NHS (2017c) *Health Visiting Programme*. Accessed on 29/10/17 at www.england.nhs.uk/ourwork/qual-clin-lead/int-rec/why

NICE (National Institute for Health and Clinical Excellence) (2015) *Children's Attachment: Attachment in Children and Young People Who Are Adopted from Care, in Care or at High Risk of Going into Care.* Available at www.nice.org.uk/guidance/ng26/resources/childrens-attachment-attachment-in-children-and-young-people-who-are-adopted-from-care-in-care-or-at-high-risk-of-going-into-care-1837335256261

NSPCC (National Society of Prevention of Cruelty to Children) (2017a) *Child Protection in the UK.* Accessed on 30/10/17 at www.nspcc.org.uk/preventing-abuse/child-protection-system

NSPCC (2017b) *Child Protection in England: Legislation, Policy and Practice.* Accessed on 30/10/17 at www.nspcc.org.uk/preventing-abuse/child-protection-system/england/legislation-policy-guidance

NSPCC (2017c) *Child Protection in Scotland: Significant Case Reviews.* Accessed on 10/4/17 at www.nspcc.org.uk/preventing-abuse/child-protection-system/scotland/significant-case-reviews

NSPCC (2017d) *Child Protection in England: Referrals and Investigations.* Accessed on 30/10/17 at www.nspcc.org.uk/preventing-abuse/child-protection-system/england/referrals-investigations

Oates, J., Karmiloff-Smith, A. and Johnson, M. (2012) *Developing Brains (Early Childhood in Focus 7).* Milton Keynes: Open University. Accessed on 12/4/17 at http://oro.open.ac.uk/33493/1/Developing_Brains.pdf

Ofsted (Office for Standards in Education) (2016) *Unknown Children – Destined for Disadvantage?* Manchester: Ofsted. Accessed on 22/10/17 at www.gov.uk/government/uploads/system/uploads/attachment_data/file/541394/Unknown_children_destined_for_disadvantage.pdf

Ofsted (Office for Standards in Education) (2017) *Childcare Providers and Inspections as at 31 March 2017.* London: Ofsted. Accessed on 8/12/17 at https://www.gov.uk/government/statistics/childcare-providers-and-inspections-as-at-31-march-2017

ONS (Office for National Statistics) (2016) 'Number of Children.' London: ONS. Accessed on 28/1/17 at www.ons.gov.uk/aboutus/transparencyandgovernance/freedomofinformationfoi/numberofchildren

Panel on Fair Access to the Professions (2009) *Unleashing Aspiration: The Final Report of the Panel on Fair Access to the Professions.* London: Cabinet Office. Accessed on 22/10/17 at http://webarchive.nationalarchives.gov.uk/+/http://www.cabinetoffice.gov.uk/media/227102/fair-access.pdf

Parton, N. and Reid, J. (2014) 'The Recent History of Central Government Guidance about Child Protection.' In S. Burton and J. Reid (eds) *Safeguarding and Protecting Children in the Early Years* (2nd edn). Abingdon: Routledge, pp.1–9.

Percival, J. (2014) 'Safeguarding within the EYFS.' In J. Reid and S. Burton (eds) *Safeguarding and Protecting Children in the Early Years* (2nd edn). Abingdon: Routledge.

Perry, B. and Szalavitz, M. (2017) *The Boy Who Was Raised as a Dog: And Other Stories from a Child Psychiatrist's Notebook – What Traumatized Children Can Teach Us About Loss, Love, and Healing* (3rd edn). New York: Basic Books.

Petrie, P., Boddy, J., Cameron, C., Wigfall, V. and Simon, A. (2006) *Working with Children in Care: European Perspectives.* Maidenhead: Open University Press/McGraw-Hill.

Plymouth Safeguarding Children Board (2010) *Serious Case Review into the Abuse at Little Ted's Nursery.* Plymouth: Plymouth Safeguarding Children Board.

Pringle, M. and Naidoo, S. (1975) *Early Child Care in Britain.* London: Gordon and Breach.

Public Health Wales (2015) *Welsh Adverse Childhood Experiences (ACE) Study. Adverse Childhood Experiences and Their Impact on Health-harming Behaviours in the Welsh Adult Population.* Wales: Public Health Wales. Accessed on 21/10/17 at www2.nphs.wales.nhs.uk:8080/PRIDDocs.nsf/7c21215d6d0c613e80256f490030c05a/d488a3852491bc1d80257f370038919e/$FILE/ACE%20Report%20FINAL%20%28E%29.pdf

QAA (Quality Assurance Agency) (2014) *Subject Benchmark Statement: Early Childhood Studies.* Accessed on 22/4/17 at www.qaa.ac.uk/en/Publications/Documents/SBS-early-childhood-studies-14.pdf

Rayns, G., Dawe, S. and Cuthbert, C. (2013) *All Babies Count: Spotlight on Drugs and Alcohol.* Accessed on 9/4/17 at www.nspcc.org.uk/globalassets/documents/research-reports/all-babies-count-spotlight-drugs-alcohol.pdf

Refuge (2017) 'The myth'. Accessed on 10/4/17 at www.refuge.org.uk/about-domestic-violence

Roberts, R. (2006) *Self-Esteem and Early Learning: Key People from Birth to School (Zero to Eight)* (3rd edn). London: Paul Chapman Publishing.

Roberts, R. (2011) *Well-being from Birth*. London: Sage.

Rose, J. and Rogers, S. (2012) *The Role of the Adult in Early Years Settings*. Maidenhead: Open University Press.

Royal College of Midwives (2017) 'Want to be a Midwife?' London: The Royal College of Midwives. Accessed on 22/7/17 at www.rcm.org.uk/learning-and-career/becoming-a-midwife

Sabates, R and Dex, S. (2012) *Multiple Risk Factors in Young Children's Development*. CLS Working Paper 2012/1. London: Centre for Longitudinal Studies. Accessed on 19/4/17 www.cls.ioe.ac.uk/shared/get-file.ashx?itemtype=document&id=1327

Siegel, D. and Bryson, T. (2011) *The Whole-brain Child: 12 Revolutionary Strategies to Nurture your Child's Developing Mind, Survive Everyday Parenting Struggles, and Help Your Family Thrive*. New York: Delacorte Press.

Siraj-Blatchford, I., Muttock, S., Sylva, K., Gilden, R. and Bell, D. (2002) *Researching Effective Pedagogy in the Early Years*. Norwich: The Stationery Office.

Schofield, G. and Beek, M. (2006) *Attachment Handbook for Foster Care and Adoption*. London: British Association for Adoption and Fostering (BAAF).

Schore, A. (2014a) 'Early interpersonal neurobiological assessment of attachment and autistic spectrum disorders.' *Frontiers in Psychology 5*, 1049, 1–13. Accessed on 26/4/17 at www.ncbi.nlm.nih.gov/pmc/articles/PMC4184129/

Schore, A. (2014b) 'Neuroscience and Attachment Theory. The Right Brain and Its Importance in the First Years.' Available at www.youtube.com/watch?v=KW-S4cyEFCc&t=1645s

Scottish Government (2017) 'Using an Adverse Childhood Experiences Tracker to Inform Targeted Support in Glasgow.' Accessed on 20/10/17 at https://education.gov.scot/improvement/Pages/sacfi7-evidence-and-data-using-adverse-childhood-experiences.aspx

Scottish Parliament (2017) *Proposed Children (Equal Protection from Assault) (Scotland) Bill*. Accessed on 21/10/17 at www.parliament.scot/parliamentarybusiness/Bills/104602.aspx

Scottish Social Services Council (2015) *Standards for Childhood Practice (2015 Revised)*. Scotland: Social Services Council. Accessed on 7/7/17 at www.sssc.uk.com/about-the-sssc/multimedia-library/publications/70-education-and-training/193-childhood-practice/244-the-standard-for-childhood-practice

Shemmings, D. and Shemmings, Y. (2011) *Understanding Disorganized Attachment: Theory and Practice for Working with Children and Adults*. London: Jessica Kingsley Publishers.

Sidebotham, P., Brandon, M., Bailey, S., Belderson, P., Dodsworth, J., Garstang, J., *et al.* (2016) *Pathways to Harm, Pathways to Protection: A Triennial Analysis of Serious Case Reviews 2011 to 2014*. Final Report. London: Department for Education. Accessed on 7/4/17 at www.gov.uk/government/uploads/system/uploads/attachment_data/file/533826/Triennial_Analysis_of_SCRs_2011-2014_-__Pathways_to_harm_and_protection.pdf

Simon, A., Hauari, H., Hollingworth, K. and Vorhaus, J. (2012) *A Rapid Literature Review of Evidence on Child Abuse Linked to Faith or Belief*. Childhood Wellbeing Research Centre. Accessed on 29/1/17 at www.gov.uk/government/uploads/system/uploads/attachment_data/file/181526/CWRC-00115-2012.pdf

Sterne, A. and Poole, L. (2010) *Domestic Violence and Children: A Handbook for Schools and Early Years Settings*. Abingdon: Routledge.

Sterne, A., Poole, L., Chadwick, D., Lawler, C. and Dodd, L.W. (2009) Domestic Violence and Children: A Handbook for Professionals Working in Schools and Early Years Settings. New York: Routledge.

Stewart, K. and Waldfogel, J. (2017) *Closing Gaps Early: The Role of Early Years Policy in Promoting Social Mobility in England*. London: The Sutton Trust. Accessed on 22/10/17 at www.suttontrust.com/wp-content/uploads/2017/09/Closing-Gaps-Early_FINAL.pdf

Taylor, I., Whiting, R. and Sharland, E. (2008) *Integrated Children's Services in Higher Education Project: Knowledge Review*. Southampton: Higher Education Academy, Social Work and Social Policy.

Taylor, J. and Thoburn, J. (2016) *Collaborative Practice with Vulnerable Children and Their Families*. London: CRC Press.

Tedam, P. and Adjoa, A. (2017) *The W Word: Witchcraft Labelling and Child Safeguarding in Social Work Practice*. St Albans: Critical Publishing.

Tinson, A., Ayrton, C., Barker, K., Born, T.B., Aldridge, H. and Kenway, P. (2016) *Monitoring Poverty and Social Inclusion 2016.* York: Joseph Rowntree Foundation (JRF). Accessed on 21/10/17 at www.jrf.org.uk/report/monitoring-poverty-and-social-exclusion-2016

UN (United Nations) (2006) *General Comment No 7 (2005). Implementing Child's Rights in Early Childhood.* New York: UN. Accessed on 13/1/17 at www2.ohchr.org/english/bodies/crc/docs/AdvanceVersions/GeneralComment7Rev1.pdf

UN (2012) *United Nations Human Rights Treaty System.* New York: UN. Accessed on 15/1/17 at www.ohchr.org/Documents/Publications/FactSheet30Rev1.pdf

UNICEF (United Nations International Children's Emergency Fund) (1989) *United Nations Convention on the Rights of the Child.* London: UNICEF. Accessed on 22/10/17 at https://www.unicef.org.uk/what-we-do/un-convention-child-rights

Ventress, N. (2014) 'Socialisation and Consequential Abuse.' In J. Reid and S. Burton (eds) *Safeguarding and Protecting Children in the Early Years* (2nd edn). Abingdon: Routledge, pp.73–91.

Wall, S., Litjens, I. and Taguma M. (2015) *Early Childhood Education and Care Pedagogy Review: England.* Paris: OECD. Accessed on 17/9/17 at www.oecd.org/unitedkingdom/early-childhood-education-and-care-pedagogy-review-england.pdf

Wave Trust (2013) *Conception to the Age of 2: The Age of Opportunity.* London: Wave Trust.

Welsh Government (2015) *Well-being of Future Generations (Wales) Act 2015.* Accessed on 18/7/17 at www.legislation.gov.uk/anaw/2015/2/contents/enacted

Wilkins, D., Shemmings, D. and Corby, B. (2012) *Child Abuse: An Evidence Base for Confident Practice* (4th edn). Maidenhead: Open University Press.

Wilkins, D., Shemmings, D. and Shemmings, Y. (2015) *A–Z of Attachment.* London: Palgrave Macmillan.

Wonnacott, J. (2013) *Serious Case Review. Under Chapter VIII 'Working Together to Safeguard Children'. In respect of the Serious Injury of Case No. 2010-11/3.* Birmingham: Birmingham Safeguarding Children Board. Accessed on 28/10/17 at www.lscbbirmingham.org.uk/images/stories/downloads/executive-summaries/Published_Overview_Report.pdf

Subject Index

Author Index

Dr Eunice Lumsden is the Head of Early Years at the University of Northampton, Fellow of the Royal Society of Arts, Senior Fellow of the Higher Education Academy and a registered social worker. Her research interests include the professionalisation of the ECEC workforce, child maltreatment, poverty and adoption. Eunice has been on the external reference groups for Early Years Professional Status and Early Years Teacher Status standards. She has advised on workforce development for the French Administration in Belgium, UNICEF in Turkey, Save the Children, the International Step by Step Association and Camden Borough Council.